Something From Nothing

Using Everyday Materials With Preschoolers

D1219220

Something From Nothing

Using Everyday Materials With Preschoolers

Emily Thompson

HIGHSCOPE
PRESS ®

Ypsilanti, Michigan

Published by

HighScope® Press

A division of the
HighScope Educational Research Foundation
600 North River Street
Ypsilanti, Michigan 48198-2898
734.485.2000, FAX 734.485.0704

Orders: 800.40.PRESS; Fax: 800.442.4FAX; www.highscope.org
E-mail: *press@highscope.org*

Copyright © 2013 by HighScope Educational Research Foundation. All rights reserved. Except as permitted under the Copyright Act of 1976, no part of this book may be reproduced or distributed in any form or by any means, electronic or mechanical, including photocopy, recording, or any information storage-and-retrieval system, without either the prior written permission from the publisher, or authorization through payment of the appropriate per-copy fee to the Copyright Clearance Center, Inc., 222 Rosewood Drive, Danvers, MA 01923, 978.750.8400, fax 978.646.8600, or on the web at www.copyright.com. The name "HighScope" and its corporate logos are registered trademarks and service marks of the HighScope Foundation.

Editor: Marcella Fecteau Weiner
Proofreader: Katie Bruckner
Cover design, text design, production: Seling Design LLC
Photography:
All photos are by Bob Foran, Ann Arbor, MI, with the following exceptions:

Gregory Fox — 8, 9, 10 (top right, bottom right), 12 (bottom right), 19, 22 (bottom), 23 (top right, bottom right), 27, 30, 38, 63 (top left, top right), 67, 89 (bottom right), 95, 150 (bottom), 157, 162, 173, 175, back cover

HighScope staff — 2, 6, 12 (bottom left), 15, 41 (bottom left, bottom right), 42, 43, 44, 52, 57, 59, 63 (bottom right), 70, 71, 81, 83, 89 (bottom left), 90, 99, 107, 137, 160, 161, 181

Kjetil Kolbjørnsrud (iStockphoto.com) — 115 (top right)

Yali Shi (iStockphoto.com) — 114 (top)

Patrick Thompson — 12 (top right), 23 (left), 69 (bottom right), 102

Library of Congress Cataloging-in-Publication Data

Thompson, Emily, 1983-
  Something from nothing using everyday materials with preschoolers / Emily Thompson.
    pages cm
  Includes bibliographical references and index.
  ISBN 978-1-57379-647-7 (soft cover : alk. paper) 1. Education, Preschool--Curricula. 2. Education, Preschool--Activity programs. I. Title.
  LB1140.4.T497 2013
  372.21--dc23

                                                              2012042423

Printed in the United States of America
10 9 8 7 6 5 4 3 2 1

Contents

Acknowledgments

We see joy and excitement in children's faces when they are playing — we can see them grow, learn, experiment, and truly be children. Watching children from different backgrounds all enjoy the same thing — play — is what inspired the creation of this book.

In 2007, I visited the Khululeka Community Education Development Centre, a HighScope Education Center in Queenstown, South Africa. The people I met there, particularly Rene King, Phakama Mzileni, and Fioni Murray, showed me how to make the fullest use of the materials you are given. These colleagues not only contributed many of the ideas in this book but also demonstrated to me their creativity with and appreciation of the materials they had at their disposal.

I am indebted to Beth Marshall, my travel partner, my mentor, the person who shaped my passion for education, and yes, my mother. We visited South Africa together and came home to create a training workshop on homemade materials. After presenting this workshop and hearing how much teachers loved the ideas, we felt a need to reach more teachers, which resulted in this book.

Many thanks to the Early Childhood staff at HighScope, who helped contribute ideas and try out materials in the HighScope Demonstration Preschool. Thanks also to Marcella Fecteau Weiner, for her support in making this book come together so nicely; Katie Bruckner, for her assistance with all aspects of the publication process; and Judy Seling, for her creativity in designing the book.

— Emily Thompson

1

Introduction

How It All Began

I became very interested in classroom materials when I visited the Khululeka Community Education Development Centre in Queenstown, South Africa, as an Early Childhood Specialist for HighScope. At Khululeka, a HighScope Education Center, I saw children and teachers using recycled, everyday materials in the most unique and interesting ways. Their use of these items seemed so clever. When I compared my experience as a preschool teacher in Michigan to what I saw in Queenstown, I realized that the focus in preschool classrooms should be on the *quality of children's experiences* with materials, rather than the materials themselves. The open-ended materials that the teachers in Queenstown found from their everyday environment truly enhanced the quality of experiences the children had in the classrooms…I was hooked!

After learning so much from Khululeka and knowing how low teachers' budgets for materials are, I knew this information had to be shared. Beth

At the Khululeka Community Education Centre in Queenstown, South Africa, teachers use everyday materials in all components of their preschool program.

Marshall (HighScope's Early Childhood Director) and I started designing a workshop that would highlight the types of materials we found at Khululeka and inform teachers of their importance in children's development. After presenting this workshop a couple of times (and having our rooms overflowing with interested teachers, hungry for materials ideas), we knew we had to write a book. We came back to our classroom at the HighScope Demonstration Preschool in Ypsilanti, Michigan, and began trying things out. Some of the ideas in this book come directly from things we saw in South Africa, some from coteachers and HighScope staff members, and some from purely playing with materials and trying things out.

Why Open-Ended Materials Are Important

Open-ended materials are materials that can be used in a variety of ways; there is no right or wrong way to play with them. Because of their flexibility, they stimulate children's thinking and grow with children as they develop. Closed-ended materials, on the other hand, have a single use or are very limited in their play possibilities; children quickly become bored with them. Once children figure out how to use a closed-ended material (which is usually not difficult), they don't have a chance to problem-solve or use their imagination. In contrast, open-ended materials enable children to use their creativity and problem-solving skills while playing with them.

With closed-ended materials, children often just have to press a button and see the action take place (e.g., dancing stuffed animals). With open-ended materials, children's play themes develop in complexity as they explore the world around them, try things out, use language in a variety of ways, and draw conclusions about how things work (or don't work). One day I observed children set up a restaurant with large hollow blocks, use an old computer keyboard as the cash register, swipe a rock down the side of the keyboard like a credit card, use some of the same rocks as food to "cook," and then serve the "food" on top of a plate at a table set with real silverware — all in the same work time! The next day at work time, I watched the children use the same hollow blocks as a boat and line up and count the same rocks in another area of the room.

According to the National Association for the Education of Young Children (2009a), it is crucial that early childhood programs give children opportunities for sustained complex play and that teachers actively support children with this type of play. Today's children often don't have the ability to play at a high level of complexity because of how they are spending their time outside of school. Thus, they lack the cognitive, social, and emotional benefits that come along with sustained complex play. Incorporating open-ended materials into the classroom is the first step in actively supporting these higher levels of play:

> They [children] learn from the concrete (e.g., manipulatives); they also apparently are capable of and interested in abstract ideas, to a far greater degree than was previously believed.... Children take all this input and work out their own understandings and hypotheses about the world. They try these out through interactions with adults and other children, physical manipulation, play, and their own thought processes — observing what happens, reflecting on their findings, imagining possibilities, asking questions, and formulating answers. When children make knowledge their own in these ways, their understanding is deeper and they can better transfer and apply their learning in new contexts. (National Association for the Education of Young Children, 2009a, pp. 108–109)

While teaching in the HighScope Demonstration Preschool, I had one particular experience that showed me how a child can learn from the concrete and apply this knowledge in a new context. Alex, a child in my class, liked to build with blocks made from small boxes. He would stack the blocks and knock them over repeatedly. Alex chose to do this almost daily for a couple of weeks. One day I was playing with some other children in the block area, where they were working hard on building a house with the hollow wooden blocks. As their structure grew in height, I noticed that it looked like it might fall over and become a safety hazard. When I told the children my concerns about their house falling over, they weren't sure how to fix the problem. I asked Alex if he could come over and help, since I knew he liked to build. Alex explained that the large blocks needed to go on the bottom and then the smaller ones could go on top; this would prevent the structure from falling over. When I asked Alex how he knew this, he told me that he likes to build towers. He then elaborated what he had learned from all his experiences with the cardboard blocks: When he built his tower with small blocks first, it fell over, but when he built it with large blocks first, he could make it a lot taller.

When children are allowed to explore and play with materials in their own ways, they build a deeper understanding of how things work. This was true for Alex — he was interested in the cardboard blocks and used them in his own way so many times that he could transfer his knowledge into new situations. As early childhood professionals, it is our job to provide materials that are interesting and engaging so that children can develop this higher level of complexity in their play.

How This Book Is Organized

Something From Nothing: Using Everyday Materials With Preschoolers focuses on open-ended materials that you can find in your everyday environment, materials that are often free (or available at a very low cost). This book is organized by categories of materials, including

- Found materials
- Natural materials
- Recycled and scrap materials
- Low-cost materials
- Easy-to-make materials

Found materials are real-life items that can be found in your everyday environment (e.g., pots and pans). **Natural materials** are items that come from nature (e.g., pine cones). **Recycled and scrap materials** are things that you use every day and should be saved for your classroom (e.g., yogurt cups). **Low-cost materials** are items that can be purchased for a small amount of money (e.g., ice cube trays and sponges). **Easy-to-make materials** use other types of materials to make classroom sets of things (e.g., sponges to make sponge balls). Many materials in this book fit in more than one category. For example, you may find rocks outside to use in your classroom (natural materials), or you may purchase rocks at a low cost at your local nursery (low-cost materials). The categories used in this book are meant to help organize the materials; they are not intended to be limiting or rigid.

Each chapter includes information on where to find the materials, where to add them in your classroom, and ideas on how to use them. The chapter on easy-to-make materials contains pictorial step-by-step directions so you can easily create a set of these materials for your classroom. Also included in each chapter are plans for small- and large-group activities that show you how to introduce and use these materials with children.

The teachers at the Khululeka Community Education Centre use various everyday materials — wood, tin cans, screws, and paint — to create a classroom set of cars.

Each small-group plan includes a scaffolding chart. The scaffolding chart contains examples of what young children at three developmental levels (earlier, middle, and later) might say and do as they engage with the materials, with corresponding examples of how you can support and gently extend learning at each level as you interact with the children. The last chapter in this book, "Involving Families," will help you talk to families about the value of open-ended materials and encourage their involvement in collecting and making these materials.

Once you have incorporated these found, natural, recycled and scrap, low-cost, and easy-to-make materials into your classroom, you will see a shift in children's play — they will become interested and curious about all the different ways they can use these materials. And we all know that when children are interested and curious, they are learning at their highest abilities.

2

Found Materials

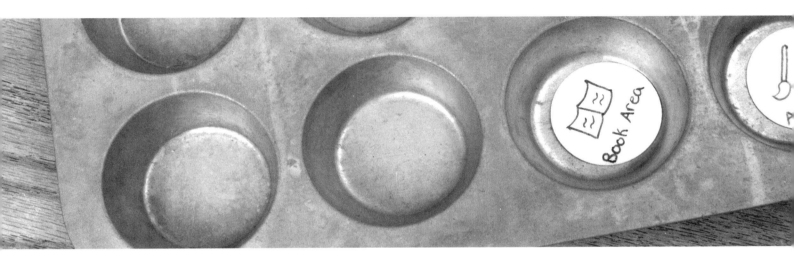

What Are Found Materials?

At work time, Matthew tells his teacher, "We are going to work." "I won-der what you are going to do at work," she replies. David, another child, says, "We are workers, so we have to do typing. But we have to get ready for work first." Matthew and David go to the house area to find neckties, which they slip over their heads. Then they get the keyboards from the shelf and take them over to the table; their teacher does the same thing. Mat-thew starts to type on his keyboard. He looks closely at the keys and says, "I found an M." David does the same and says, "I found my D." Both boys and the teacher continue to name letters and push the corresponding keys.

Found materials are exactly that — materials that you can find in your every-day environment. They are real objects that are commonly found and used in our homes, cars, workplaces, garages, and other places you frequent daily.

Found materials are indispensable in the preschool classroom. Children love to mimic the adults they see in their lives and play out the situations that are familiar to them (such as going to the doctor or making dinner). Using real (found) materials to enhance this kind of play is much more appealing to children than giving them fake, plastic toys that represent the real materials. Holding a hefty, heavy metal pot that looks and feels like the pots at home is more satisfying than holding a plastic, neon-colored fake! In addition, children can use found mate-rials in the classroom in many different ways, from pretending to call a parent at work with an old cell phone to finding the letters in their name on a keyboard. Finally, found materials are a great value to teachers. They last a lot lon-ger than plastic toys, and teachers can usually find found materials at a low cost or, even bet-ter, for free (Epstein & Hohmann, 2012).

Neckties are a great addition to the house area for dress-up play.

Real materials (e.g., heavy metal pots) encourage children to play out situations that are familiar to them, such as making dinner.

Where Do I Add Found Materials in My Classroom?

Found materials, like any materials in a preschool classroom, should be stored with similar items. For example, store all items to eat with (e.g., plates, silverware, and cups) on the same shelf or all car-type items (e.g., steering wheels and keys) in the same place. Place the materials in areas based on the play happening there. If, for example, the children in your classroom do a lot of counting in the toy area, add poker chips there, or if they are pretending to cook in the house area, add the poker chips in a food canister to that area.

Found materials in the interest areas

On page 11 are some examples of found materials and the areas in your classroom where you might find them. As you will note, some of these materials are listed in more than one area (such as pots and pans in the house area as well as the outdoor play space); you may decide to provide them in one or more places or simply rotate them into different areas, depending on the play happening in your classroom at a given time. For example, if the children are always bringing the poker chips from the toy area into the house area, store the poker chips in the house area, where the children are using them the most.

Found Materials in Classroom Areas

Steering wheels in the block area

Measuring cups in the sand and water area

Cooking utensils in the house area

Hammers in the woodworking area

In the House Area

- Pots and pans
- Silverware
- Cash register
- Credit card machine
- Luggage
- Lunchboxes
- Dishes and cups
- Mixing bowls
- Measuring cups
- Utensils
- Dress-up clothes
- Shoes
- Broom and dust pan
- Dusters
- Dust buster (a nonworking one)
- Empty laundry bottles
- Iron (with the cord cut off)
- Old cell phones
- Keyboards
- Phones
- Empty food boxes and containers

In the Block Area

- Steering wheel
- Car dials
- Keys
- Nuts and bolts

In the Toy Area

- Poker chips
- Cookie sheets (used as magnet story boards; see p. 152)

- Keys
- Ice cube trays (to sort items in)
- Muffin tins (to sort items in)
- Letters from a Scrabble or Boggle game
- Dice

In the Sand and Water Area

- Measuring cups
- Spoons
- Plastic food containers
- Mixing bowls

In the Woodworking Area

- Hammers
- Nails
- Screwdrivers
- Screws
- Hand drills
- Wood
- Golf tees

In the Outside Play Space

- Pots and pans
- Utensils
- Silverware
- Measuring cups
- Cell phones
- Steering wheels
- Car dials

Found Materials for Play Themes

This child takes her "puppy" on a walk using a dog leash. The "puppy" stops to beg for the bone his owner is carrying.

Using real preemie diapers, this teacher helps a child diaper her "baby."

These two children play out a camping scenario with a small pop-up tent.

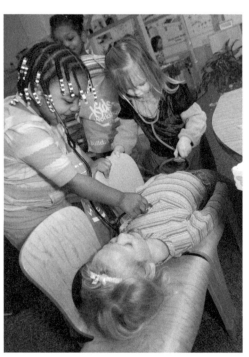

These "doctors" use real stethoscopes (donated by a parent who is a doctor) to figure out what is wrong with their "sick patient."

Found materials for natural play themes

You can add found materials to your learning environment on a temporary basis, based on the natural play themes that are happening in your classroom at a given time. For example, if children have just returned from a family camping trip and are playing out this theme during work time, you might add a pop-up tent and sleeping bags to your block area. Some examples of play themes and the materials to add are listed here:

For a Camping Play Theme

- Small pop-up tent
- Sleeping bags
- Small cooler
- Flashlights
- Camping-type food containers (e.g., canteens, mess kits)
- Compass

For a Doctor's Office Play Theme

- Stethoscopes
- Old x-rays
- Ace bandages
- Old air casts
- Slings

For a Beauty/Barber Shop Play Theme

- Blow dryer (with the cord cut off)
- Curling iron (with the cord cut off)
- Straightener (with the cord cut off)
- Hair clips
- Headbands
- Combs
- Brushes
- Hair ties
- Smocks
- Empty shampoo bottles
- Velcro hair rollers

For a Baby Play Theme

- Preemie clothes with snaps and zippers
- Preemie diapers (with Velcro)
- Socks
- Hats
- Bibs
- Bottles
- Baby dishes
- Baby blankets
- Rattles

For a Travel Play Theme[1]

- Luggage
- Passport holders
- Wallets
- Purses
- Sunglasses

---

[1]Adapted from Henderson (1991).

- Small travel-sized containers for toiletries
- Travel brochures
- Maps

For a Restaurant Play Theme
- Menus
- Cooking materials (e.g., pots and pans, dishes, utensils)
- Fast-food bags and containers
- Order pads
- Bank/change envelopes
- Place mats
- Uniforms (e.g., a McDonald's shirt, waiter/waitress uniform, Pizza Hut hat, visors)
- Aprons

For a Dog and/or Cat Play Theme
- Leashes
- Pet dishes
- Dog bones
- Clean dog/cat toys
- Pet beds

For a Beach Play Theme
- Blankets
- Towels
- Beach balls
- Sunglasses
- Sun hats
- Empty sunscreen bottles
- Small cooler

Found materials that reflect the community

When adding found materials to your classroom, think about items that relate to the local community and its events, cultures, and traditions. Before adding found materials that reflect your children and their families to your classroom environment, get to know the families in your program. One way of doing this is to visit the children and their families in their home at the beginning of the school year. These home visits are a great opportunity to get to know the child and the family on a more personal level.

You can also give each family a beginning-of-the-year "family survey" to find out more about the child and his or her family (e.g., ask about other family members, family pets, a child's favorite interests, and so forth).

Bright Idea
Holiday Visitors

For a small-group time in December, have a parent that is familiar with one of the holidays celebrated at this time come join your small group.

For example, for Hanukkah, ask the parent to show the children the dreidel game at the opening of small-group time. Then give the children dreidels and coins. Children can choose to play this game, make up their own game using the dreidel and coins, or just practice spinning dreidels! For the ending of your small-group time, tell the children that you will add the dreidels to the house area for the next day.

On this survey be sure to ask families to share any home traditions or cultural experiences that they would like to share with the class. Ask families about community events that are important to them (e.g., a veterans' parade or an annual festival that celebrates their heritage), remembering that every home is different and differences among children's family backgrounds need to be respected and valued. Be sure, therefore, to acknowledge various experiences and differences in children's lives in the materials you choose for the classroom setting.

Here are some things to think about when adding found materials that reflect the community:

For Traditions

- Christmas
  - Small Christmas tree
  - Wrapping paper
  - Christmas cookie cutters with play dough

- Hanukkah
  - Dreidels
  - Menorah

- Kwanzaa
  - Mat (mkeka)
  - Candle holder (kinara)
  - Unity cup (kikombe cha umoja)

- Ramadan
  - Traditional lanterns for Ramadan (fanoos)

- Chinese New Year
  - Small red envelopes (hong bao) with coins (ya sui qian)
  - Bubble wrap (to be stomped on to simulate the sound of firecrackers)
  - Dragon puppets (for dragon parade)

- Diwali (Festival of Lights)
  - Candle holder (diya)
  - Different-sized boxes wrapped (for gifts)
  - Construction paper and crayons to make cards for Diwali

This child builds his train track around the Christmas tree (to be decorated by the children during work time).

For Events
- Harvest
  - Pumpkins
  - Corn on the cob; corn in the sensory table
  - Berries
- Items used during different cultural festivals (e.g., Cinco de Mayo, Irish dancing, mid-autumn [Chinese lunar] festival, Mardi Gras, Polish festival, pow-wows)

For Different Cultures
- Traditional clothing
- Traditional shoes

- Authentic decorations for celebrations (see **For Traditions** on p. 15 for additional ideas)

For Your Local Environment
- Outdoor gear (e.g., snow shoes if you live in a cold environment, hiking boots if you live in a mountainous area, diving fins/snorkel masks if you live by the ocean)
- Bus passes
- Cowboy boots
- Horse shoes
- Train tickets
- Subway tickets or tokens

Where Do I Find Found Materials?

So where can you get found materials? Put on your collecting hat and save almost everything you come in contact with, starting with your own home. Instead of throwing away that outdated cell phone, take it into your classroom. Don't have that huge garage sale with old clothes and worn pots and pans — put them in your house area. Be on the lookout at resale shops and garage sales, and ask everyone you know to save things for you. The dollar store is another great place to look for inexpensive found materials.

Some found materials don't have to be donated for good; they can just be borrowed for a period of time. For example, if it is summertime and children are talking about family camping trips, borrow your sister's pop-up tent for a few weeks so the children can play with it in your classroom and bring it back home when they are done.

Found materials are also great items to ask for from your families. Most families can usually find old things in their basements or storage areas that they never knew what to do with; just make a list of items that you would like for your classroom and send it home with the children in your program.

When looking for found materials, keep in mind the safety of the items. Instead of china dishes that are easily breakable, look for dishes that are made of heavy, durable plastic. Always cut off the cords on old items, because they can be choking or electrical hazards. Watch for sharp items such as knives or other things with blades; choose dull butter knives for your house area. When working with younger children, look for small parts and pieces that may come off the items. Finally, be sure to wash clothes and thoroughly clean materials before placing them in the classroom.

What Can I Do With Found Materials?

Found materials help children develop deeper and more complex play. If children are given real, authentic materials, they can add realistic details to their play — instead of simply using plastic food for their restaurant, children can take orders from a menu, write the orders on a service pad, and/or "cook" the food with real pots and utensils. Instead of having only plastic dishes to place on the table, children can set the table with real place mats, dishes, and sil-

Using a kitchen frying pan and spatula, this child cooks up some tasty "food" and serves it on real plates.

verware. You can support this type of complex play by providing children with interesting found materials that are consistent with the play currently happening in the classroom.

Using found materials for pretend play

Children often use found materials throughout the classroom for pretend play, as props in their play situations. They imitate actions and language of others by playing out what they see happening in their everyday lives, as shown in the following examples:

Keisha and Mallory build a McDonald's drive-through with hollow blocks and make up Happy Meals with the McDonald's bags and chicken-nugget cartons. "You be the orderer and I am the cook," says Keisha to Mallory.

At work time in the block area, Juan builds a truck with some boxes. He gets the steering wheel and gears off the shelf and adds them to his "truck." Then he brings a trash can over and places it on the back of his truck. When asked about his truck, Juan replies that he is a garbage man like his dad and is going to get his "uniform" on. He proceeds to the house area and puts on a workman's shirt.

Bright Idea
Planning With Muffin Tins

Have you thought about using those muffin tins for planning time? Draw your area signs on sticky notes, stick each note in a different section of the tin, and then give children a pine cone (or something similar). Ask the children to put their pine cone in the section with the corresponding area sign of where they want to play and tell you their plan.

Using found materials to support curriculum content

Pretend play is what you'll see most when children use found materials, but children use found materials in lots of other ways as well. You'll see children *ordering* the measuring cups or spoons and mixing bowls by size; *counting* train tickets and corn kernels or pumpkin seeds; *identifying letters* on menus or cookbooks; *filling and emptying* plastic drinking cups (and learning about spatial awareness along the way); *reading* familiar words on food boxes and restaurant menus; *developing their fine-motor skills* when using real clothes to dress themselves or dolls; and *classifying* keys by color, as Sonja demonstrates:

Sonja dumps out a basket of keys in the toy area. She then sorts the keys into two piles, silver keys and gold keys. "Look," she says, "there are more gold ones."

When children have materials in the classroom that mimic real materials from their homes, they see that their cultures and family backgrounds are respected and accepted in the classroom. Including materials that are familiar to children's everyday environments also helps them develop a positive self-identity. In addition, children's language increases when they are playing out something that is familiar and interesting to them and when they have an engaged partner to listen to and participate in the dialogue (Epstein, 2012).

This found material — a restaurant menu — is a great conversation starter. "What would you like?" asks the child. "Hmm...let's see what my options are," answers the teacher, as they look at the menu together.

How Do I Use These Materials With Children?

In addition to giving children those intriguing experiences in our classrooms by adding found materials throughout, we also need to make sure to engage with children as they use these materials. Try following these steps[2] for participating in children's play.

Look for natural play openings

Wait until you see a natural opening to join children's exploratory play, pretend play, games, and constructive play. Here is an example of how a teacher waits until she sees an opening to join in a pretend-play scenario:

Beth, a teacher, observes Hallie and Robert calling each other on cell phones and asking each other about how much candy they received from Halloween the previous day. When Beth sees a natural pause in the conversation, she picks up another cell phone; "calls" Hallie and Robert; and says, "I got M&M's for Halloween — they are my favorite!"

Join children's play on their level

This may mean squatting, kneeling, sitting (as Lynne does in the following anecdote), and occasionally even lying on the floor:

Spencer and Meiko build a "car" out of large hollow blocks, car dials, and a steering wheel. They invite Lynne, a teacher, to join them. Lynne sits down on one of the blocks so that she is "in the car" with the children and pretends to go on a trip with them.

By playing on the children's level, the children are not "looking up" to you and you are not "looking down" on them.

---

[2]These steps are adapted from HighScope Educational Research Foundation (2011).

Play in parallel with children

This strategy can be effective during exploratory play, as the adult plays near the child using the same materials in the same or similar manner:

Eliza is poking golf tees into a piece of Styrofoam repeatedly when Mary, a teacher, gets her own piece of Styrofoam and mimics Eliza's actions. Eliza watches Mary doing this and says, "I like the sound it makes."

Play as a partner with children

This works well with children involved in pretend play or games, with adults functioning as equals and followers, as Jill does here:

While Beau and Mason are pretending to have a picnic outside with plates, silverware, a blanket, and pea gravel, Jill, a teacher, comes over and sits on the blanket with them. She says, "I am really hungry." Mason replies, "Here is a sandwich for you; it's peanut butter and jelly." Jill pretends to eat the "sandwich" and have a picnic with the boys.

Refer one child to another

Referring children to one another encourages them to recognize each other's strengths and use them to help others, see each other as valuable resources, and play cooperatively:

Addison packs a suitcase full of a pretend passport, dress-up clothes, a map, and sunglasses. She approaches Elizabeth, a teacher, and says, "I am ready to go on my trip, but I don't know where to go." Elizabeth replies, "Hmm…well, I remember Drew went on a trip yesterday. Maybe you could ask him for an idea." Addison goes to Drew (who was watching close by) and the two of them pretend to go on a trip to Hawaii.

See the following two pages for pictorial examples of how adults participate in children's play.

How Adults Participate in Children's Play

Look for natural play openings. *"Can I give you a cookie?" asks the adult, as she hands this child a "cookie" (a crayon) as part of their pretend-play mealtime.*

Join children's play on their level. *After officiating a wedding between this boy and his bride, the teacher (otherwise known as the wedding officiator) and the bride and her sister go home to rest, while the husband goes off to work.*

Play as a partner with children. *This teacher participates with the children's pretend play as she joins in for a group photo.*

Play in parallel with children. *This adult works alongside the child as he plays with Magna-Tiles and bottle caps.*

Refer one child to another. *Andrew wants to take apart the watches (the teachers collected broken watches from families at the beginning of the year) but isn't sure where to start. "I wonder what Brian is doing," this teacher says to Andrew as she points to the watch that Brian is hammering.*

Activities for Found Materials

Let's Have a Birthday Party

Children use found materials to have a pretend birthday party.

Time of day

Small-group time

Content areas

- Creative Arts
- Language, Literacy, and Communication

Materials

For each child and teacher:

- A plate, cup, fork, and butter knife
- Play dough
- Basket to hold above materials

Shared materials:

- None

Backup materials:

- Birthday decorations (e.g., birthday hats, signs, candles, table centerpieces)

Beginning

- Start by asking the children, "Has anyone ever been to a birthday party before?" Listen to their answers, and talk with the children about their experiences at birthday parties.

- Get children's ideas about what happens at birthday parties. You might ask, for example, "What do you do at a birthday party? What do you eat?"

- Give each child a basket with plates, cups, silverware, and play dough, and then say something like "I wonder what you are going to do with these materials to get ready for a birthday party."

Middle

- Encourage children to look at their materials and think about their birthday experiences. Make some birthday food yourself with your materials and talk about what you are doing. You might say, for example, "I like hot dogs at parties" while you roll your play dough into the shape of a hot dog.

- Walk around to each child to talk about what he or she is doing and making with the materials. Converse with the children about their birthday experiences. Offer them birthday decorations if they seem to be done with the other materials.

End

- As children are finishing, sing the birthday song together, and then let them know that they have five minutes to finish their birthday food.

- Have the children transition to the next part of your routine by singing the birthday song, placing four children in each round. Sing, for example, "Happy birthday to Matthew, happy birthday to Ella, happy birthday to Josh, happy birthday to John," and then repeat the song until all the children have transitioned.

Ideas for follow-up

- Place the birthday materials in the house area.

- During recall time, use the birthday hat as a prop — the child wearing the birthday hat recalls.

- Add birthday invitations to your classroom along with a class list nearby so that children can choose to write invitations to their classmates.

Adaptations for children with special needs

- To help improve children's fine-motor strength, encourage them to squeeze, pinch, press, and smooth the play dough with their fingertips.

After making a birthday cake from play dough, this child uses the knife to cut pieces so she can share her cake with classmates.

Developmental Range for "Let's Have a Birthday Party": Supporting Children at Different Levels

Earlier	Middle	Later
Children may	*Children may*	*Children may*
• Use plates, cups, silverware, and play dough.	• Explain their play in more detail (e.g., say "I am making a cupcake for the party" and then use the play dough to represent the cupcake).	• Role-play the birthday party and make items for the party with other children.
• Shape the play dough somehow but not be sure about what it is yet.	• Ask questions related to birthday parties.	• Start to "decorate" for the party and have a common theme among each other.
• Say a few words about what they are doing.		• Talk with other children or an adult about birthday parties as part of a conversation.
Adults can	*Adults can*	*Adults can*
• Mimic the children's actions with the materials (e.g., if a child flattens play dough and then uses the silverware to cut it up, do the same with their materials).	• Listen to the children's ideas about what they are making or playing out and answer their questions.	• Help children set up their party.
• Encourage the children to share about their own birthdays. For example, if a child says, "Mommy makes me pancakes on my birthday," say "I wonder how we could make a pancake with our dough."	• Talk to the children about what else they have seen at birthday parties and inquire how they can add these ideas to what they are doing.	• Engage in conversation with the children and join their birthday party play.
• Listen to children's birthday ideas, repeating their words.	• Share their own birthday experiences with children.	• Inquire about more details of their party and see if children join in on the ideas. You might say, for example, "I see you have a cake with candles. What else could your party have?"

Take Me for a Ride

Children sing and act out the song "Car-Car" (by Woody Guthrie).

Time of day

Large-group time

Content areas

- Creative Arts
- Physical Development and Health

Materials

For each child and teacher:

- Key
- Large, hollow wooden block (or sturdy crates or chairs) to sit on

Shared materials:

- Steering wheel
- Basket (for cleanup)

Backup materials:

- None

Beginning

- Teach the children "Car-Car" by having them repeat the lines of the first stanza to you.
- Tell the children that you are going to pretend to go for a ride on different vehicles (e.g., plane, boat, car, truck, bus). Give each child a hollow block and a key.
- Have children sit on their blocks and use their keys to start their vehicles.

Middle

- Sing "Car-Car" with the children.
- Give each child a chance to change the type of vehicle in "Car-Car." The child whose turn it is to choose the vehicle can use the steering wheel and pretend to drive the rest of the class.
- Encourage the children to use their keys to start their vehicles each time the song is sung.

End

- Tell the children that you have time to sing the song once more, and ask them to place their keys in a basket and stack their blocks up while singing the song.
- After cleanup, sing the song again, adding in the next part of your daily routine (e.g., "Take me for a ride to snack, snack").

Ideas for follow-up

- Add keys and steering wheels to the block area.

- Add the song "Car-Car" to the class's songbook (you don't always have to use the props; you can simply sing the song together).

Adaptations for children with special needs

- If a child cannot sit on a hollow block, use a carpet square instead (a carpet square may be easier to sit on since it requires no balance). A child using a wheelchair could also be wheeled on top of a carpet square.

As a follow-up to this activity, children use the steering wheel as a prop for planning time — the children "drive" to where they plan to go for work time.

Scrabble Letters

Children identify letters and start to build words.

Time of day

Small-group time

Content areas

- Language, Literacy, and Communication

Materials

For each child and teacher:

- Letters from Scrabble or Boggle game (be sure to give children the letters in their names) in a basket
- Cookie sheet

Shared materials:

- Extra Scrabble letters

Backup materials:

- Class list
- Marker and small pieces of paper

Beginning

- Tell the children that today they are going to be looking for letters that are in their names.

- Show the children the Scrabble letters. Demonstrate how they can take the letters out of their baskets and place them on the cookie sheets (this defines a place to work and will help children group their letters).

- Begin to use your letters to spell your name, and describe what you are doing. For example, you might pick up the letter *E* and then say, "I found my letter *E*, the first letter in my name. I am going to place it on my cookie sheet and look for my next letter."

- Give each child his or her own basket of letters and a cookie sheet.

Middle

- Walk around the children as they are using the letters. Support their work by naming the letters they have pulled out or by asking them to tell you what letters they have found.

- If children are interested in finding their classmates' letters, show them the class list to help them find the letters in their names (and maybe put them together).

- Some children might be interested in making words with the letters. Use the small pieces of paper and marker to write these words so that the children can independently look for the letters.

End

- Give children a time warning that the activity will be ending soon. After that amount of time has passed, tell the children that you will add the letters to the toy area for the next day.
- Have children put their cookie sheets in a stack and their letters in a bin.
- Transition the children to the next part of your daily routine by pulling out a letter, and then say "If your name starts with this letter, move to large-group time." Continue until all the children have transitioned to the next activity.

Ideas for follow-up

- Put children's first letter of their names in a cup. Ask a child to pull out a letter from the cup; the child whose letter it is can take a turn to plan or recall.
- Place the letters in a basket in the toy area with the cookie sheets close by.
- If children enjoy looking for letters, have them go on a letter hunt around your classroom. Give them small pads of paper and pencils to write down all the letters that they find.

Developmental Range for "Scrabble Letters": Supporting Children at Different Levels

Earlier	Middle	Later
Children may	*Children may*	*Children may*
• Collect letters and misname them.	• Identify more letters.	• Find all the letters in their name and place them on the cookie sheets.
• Find the first letter in their name.	• Find some letters in their names.	• Put together simple words on their cookie sheets.
	• Find letters and identify the child or adult whose name starts with that letter.	
Adults can	*Adults can*	*Adults can*
• Help children with the correct names of the letters by saying something like "I see you found an *A, H,* and a *K.*"	• Repeat the letters that children have found.	• State what they see children doing (e.g., "I see you found all your letters").
• Help children find a familiar letter that they know.	• Sound out the letters that a child has already found (e.g., say "I see you found an *A* for Allie").	• Help children put together a word by writing the word on a piece of paper.
• Ask children if they can find another letter in their name (and perhaps give them their written name to look at while they find the letters).	• Help children realize the other letters in children's names by using a class list or paper and markers.	• Ask children to find all of the letters in their name and a classmate's name (note that children may need help sounding out names).
	• Help children find all the letters in their names by saying something like "I see you found a *T*, two *N*s, and an *R* for your name. I wonder where the *A* and *E* are."	

Caring for Baby

Children pretend to care for baby dolls using real baby clothes and items.

Time of day

Small-group time

Content areas

- Social and Emotional Development
- Creative Arts
- Physical Development and Health

Materials

For each child and teacher:

- Baby doll
- Preemie diaper
- Onesie
- Socks
- Hat
- Basket to hold above materials

Shared materials:

- Baskets (to sort baby clothes for cleanup)

Backup materials:

- Bottle
- Baby blanket
- Other baby items (e.g., rattles, pacifiers, baby dishes)

Beginning

- Start by talking to the children about their experiences with babies (perhaps some children have younger siblings or cousins). Converse with them about babies and what they need and what they do.
- Tell the children that today you have some babies that need to be taken care of. Give each child a basket with the materials for this activity.

Middle

- Visit with each child, commenting on what you see the child doing with the doll and baby materials.
- If children need assistance dressing their baby, talk them through the process slowly, pointing out each step that needs to be taken. You might say, for example, "First lay the diaper out and place the baby on top. Then bring the flap [point out the flap to the child] up and Velcro the side."
- Pass out backup materials to those children who are ready for them.

End

- Give children a warning that the activity will be ending soon.
- Ask children to sort baby clothes into separate baskets.

- Tell the children that the babies and materials will be available to use in the house area.

- Ask the children to crawl like babies to the next part of the daily routine.

Ideas for follow-up

- To add a fine-motor challenge, put up a clothesline where children can hang the baby clothes with clothespins.

- Place washcloths and baby soap bottles in the house area.

Adaptations for children with special needs

- Some children may have a hard time fastening baby clothes that have snaps because this requires fine-motor strength. Try to find some clothes that fasten with Velcro, which may be easier for children to do at first.

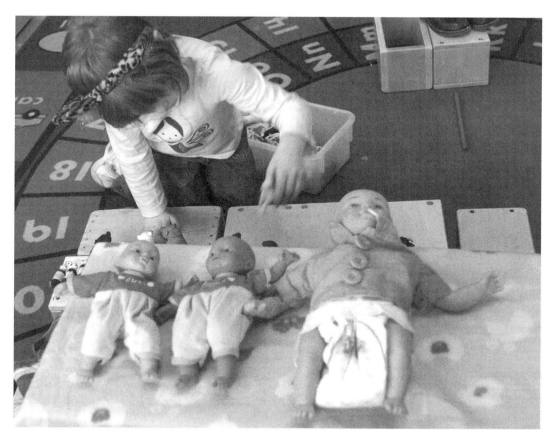

After this small-group time, this young child continues to play with the baby dolls, lining them up by size.

Developmental Range for "Caring for Baby": Supporting Children at Different Levels

Earlier	Middle	Later
Children may	*Children may*	*Children may*
• Have a hard time dressing their baby. • Dress the baby and then use some materials with the baby (but not verbally pretend with materials).	• Dress the baby but have a difficult time with the fasteners on the clothing. • Pretend with the materials, using some language while pretending (e.g., say "Drink your milk" to the baby).	• Dress their baby and fasten the clothes by themselves. • Pretend with the materials, using lots of language (e.g., "We need to get you dressed because it is time for bed. Let's get on your pajamas").
Adults can	*Adults can*	*Adults can*
• Slowly describe the steps taken when dressing their doll. • Acknowledge children's feelings (e.g., "You seem like you are getting frustrated"). • Comment on what a child is doing with the materials (e.g., "I see you are using the bottle to feed your baby").	• Acknowledge children's feelings and offer help when children are too frustrated or upset. • Engage in children's pretend play with them. • Follow children's leads and mimic their play ideas.	• Engage in children's play with them. • Converse with children about their knowledge of babies, adding comments and ideas when appropriate.

3

Natural Materials

What Are Natural Materials?

While playing in the house area, Jayla explains to Kovid that she is having a restaurant and he can buy something if he wants. Kovid says he would like a piece of pizza. Jayla uses the play dough to make a flat circle and then places rocks on top as slices of pepperoni. Kovid takes the pizza, and Jayla says, "That will be five dollars please." Kovid replies, "I don't have any money, just a card," and hands her a seashell. Jayla takes the shell; runs it down the side of the table; hands it back to Kovid; and says, "Thanks. Have a nice day."

Natural materials are materials you (and the children) find in nature, such as leaves, acorns, shells, rocks, and snow, to name just a few.

When thinking about nature, we tend to think about playing on the playground at outside time, going on outdoor field trips, and taking walks outside. Although these experiences are important for children so that they can explore the outdoors, be physically active, appreciate nature, and respect the environment, we also want to think about bringing the outdoors (and the materials it

Bringing natural items inside the classroom allows children to become more familiar with materials that are available outside the classroom.

offers) into the classroom. Bringing these types of natural materials into the classroom allows children to become more familiar with materials that are available in the outdoor space.

Where Do I Add Natural Materials in My Classroom?

Sort your natural materials so that there is one type of material in each container; for example, rocks, twigs, leaves, and pebbles should all be stored in separate containers (or bins or canisters). Make sure that children have easy access to the containers so that they can be independent users of the materials.

Storage and presentation are also very important — a dirty bin with crumpled-up dead leaves is not appealing to anyone, especially children. Be sure to throw out natural materials that have broken down over time and replace them with colorful materials that are still intact. No matter what material we are thinking about, present them in ways that will captivate children.

Natural materials are extremely open ended; one day a piece of bark is a credit card and the next day it becomes the wall of a doghouse. Since these materials are so open ended, simply placing them in interest areas will encourage children to use them in many different ways, and you'll find that these natural materials will migrate from one area to the next.

On the following page are examples of natural materials and the areas in your classroom that you might find them.

When storing and presenting natural materials in your preschool classroom, be sure to discard materials that have broken down over time (e.g., pine cones, dead leaves) and replace them with new ones.

In the House Area

- Shells
- Rocks
- Flowers

In the Block Area

- Driftwood
- Tree slices (thin stumps)

In the Toy Area

- Pine cones
- Acorns
- Shells
- Rocks

In the Sand and Water Area

- Pebbles
- Dirt
- Sand
- Water
- Seed pods
- Grasses and moss
- Straw
- Snow

In the Art Area

- Sticks and twigs
- Feathers
- Clay
- Leaves
- Pine needles
- Nuts (only use if children in your program do not have nut allergies)
- Bark
- Flowers
- Straw
- Sea weed/sea grass

In the Outside Play Space

- Tree stumps
- Tree slices (thin stumps)
- Logs
- Boulders

Where Do I Find Natural Materials?

To find these materials, you will have to put on your explorer hat and get dirty. Well, perhaps you don't really have to get dirty, but finding these materials is more fun when you get to play with them yourself! That said, items from nature are easy to collect. Take a walk around the school building with your children to collect these items in bags, and ask families to bring these items into class. Keep an eye out for these items around your own home as well. As these materials are coming from our natural environment, make sure you (and the children) find them on the ground so that no one is disturbing nature.

Natural Materials in Classroom Areas

Shells in the toy area

Tree slices (thin stumps) in the outside play space

Dirt in the sand and water area

Acorns in the house area

You can also purchase many of these materials for a low cost at different stores, including craft stores, which sell seashells, rocks, and pine cones as decorative items for vases or bowls (be sure they are not fragranced or treated with toxic materials). This is a resourceful way to get natural materials that you might not find in your local environment.

What Can I Do With Natural Materials?

According to Zach Pine, an artist and educator, "The most important thing is to provide natural materials, like rocks, twigs, leaves, or pine cones, then invite and permit learners to be creative. No matter where they live or learn, everyone has a connection with nature" (Rose, 2011, para. 6). Natural materials foster a greater understanding of the world around us, and we want children to be able to explore and investigate different materials, and experiment with what they can do. By integrating natural materials into all parts of your environment, you'll see children use these materials in many different ways.

Using natural materials for art

Natural materials can be used for art, as an alternative to traditional art supplies or as the focus of an art activity itself:

Luke lightly moves his feather in and out of the paint on his paper, making a very light stroke.

After collecting leaves at outside time, children choose to use them again at work time. Some children place their leaves under paper and use crayons to do leaf rubbings. Another child glues some leaves on a recycled shoebox and says he is making a "leaf box to collect more leaves in."

Bright Idea
Small-Group Times

Natural materials are great to use with other materials for small-group times. Try using rocks and play dough or rocks, nuts, and a magnifying glass for a small-group time to see what the children do.

This young girl sorts her rocks into three piles (by size) during a small-group time.

Using natural materials during play

You might see the children using natural materials, such as branches and grass, for their pretend-play scenarios, as illustrated in the following anecdotes:

Mia and Annie pretend to go camping in the block area. They collect some branches from the art area, pile them up on the floor, and call them their "campfire."

In Bryce and Kiefer's preschool class, the children grow grass together in the sand and water table. When the grass is too tall, Bryce and Kiefer cut the grass and use it with their animal figures.

Children will also order and compare natural materials, as Amelia and Mason demonstrate:

Amelia sorts her rocks into two piles and says, "These ones are black and these ones are brown." Mason lines his rocks up from smallest to largest. He says, "Now they are in order."

Using natural materials in the outdoor play space

Tree stumps, slices, and logs are great for your outdoor play space — children can use them to balance on, jump off, pretend with around the space, and sort and stack, as Marcus demonstrates:

While playing outside, Marcus gets the bin of tree slices. He starts stacking the slices with the largest on the bottom and then places the next smallest on top until he has a stack from largest to smallest.

You can also convert tree stumps into tables and chairs (where children can sit and play with materials) by placing a board on top of an old tree stump (for the table) and then add two more tree stumps next to the table as chairs.

As with any material teachers provide in the classroom, adults need to engage with children as they use the materials in their own ways. For tips on how to participate in children's play, see "How Do I Use These Materials With Children?" on pages 20–21.

These children remove the bark from a recently downed tree and explore what they find under it.

A Nature Activity Bag

Does your classroom or school have a lending library so families can borrow and return classroom books? You can also create a lending library for activity bags. A lending library for activity bags works in much the same way, except its purpose is to loan out materials for activities that families can do at home together.

Activity bags can have anything you want in them, such as a small set of toys, a recipe idea, a card game, a book with a corresponding activity, or a description of a physical activity for a family to do together. Families can sign them out for several days or a week at a time.

To create a nature activity bag, put the following in a large, resealable bag:

- A book about nature with lots of pictures (guidebooks work great)

- White glue

- Paper or cardboard (for collage)

- Card with instructions for the family (see box below to copy and put in nature activity bag)

Nature Hunt

1. **Designate a nature area.** Go on a walk around the block or go to a local park.

2. **Take with you.** Take along some bags so you can bring home natural materials and the included nature book.

3. **Collect.** Walk around your designated nature area, and pick up natural materials on the ground that would be fun to use for a collage at home and in the classroom (e.g., pine cones, leaves, sticks, flowers).

4. **Make it fun.** Try to find some of the same materials that are shown in the nature book.

5. **Do.** Make a natural material collage with white glue and paper when you get back home.

6. **Share.** Bring your extra materials into the classroom to add to our art area.

Copyright © 2013 HighScope® Educational Research Foundation. The owner of this book has permission to copy this card for its use in an early childhood program.

Activities for Natural Materials

Story Can: Walking Through the Woods

Children use materials from nature to tell simple stories.

Time of day

Small-group time

Content areas

- Language, Literacy, and Communication
- Creative Arts

Materials

For each child and teacher:

- Tin can containing
  - Blue fabric or paper
  - 2 to 3 small people figures
  - 1 or 2 pine cones
  - 4 to 6 pebbles
  - 3 or 4 sticks

Shared materials:

- None

Backup materials:

- None

Beginning

- Start the small group by opening your own story can and pulling out the materials.

- Tell a short story using the materials in your story can. For example, you might say, "Once upon a time there was a boy [the boy person figure] who was going on a walk through the woods. He had to move around all the tall trees [the pine cones] and over lots of tiny sticks [the sticks]. Then he came across some rocks [the pebbles] and heard some splashing noises. He looked over the rocks and saw a beautiful lake [blue fabric or paper]."

- Say to the children "I have some story cans for you. I wonder what kind of story you are going to tell." Give each child a story can.

At the beginning of this small-group time, each child receives a story can that contains the materials for this activity.

Middle

- Listen to the children's stories, repeating some of the vocabulary they are using.

- Look for a natural play opening and join children's play in pretending with a person figure from your story can. Stay in character and follow children's leads.

End

- Give the children a time warning before the end of the activity.

- Ask the children to place all their materials back in their tins, and remind them where they can find similar natural materials in the classroom (you can take the materials out of the tins and sort them into different containers in the classroom).

- Tell a story as a way to transition children to the next part of the routine. For example, you might tell a story such as this: "Once upon a time there were eight children who were very hungry. Those eight children had to get up and wash their hands before they could eat. So they all stood up and tiptoed through their classroom to the sinks to wash their hands."

Ideas for follow-up

- On the message board, remind children of where the natural materials are in the classroom.

- Go on a walk and see if the children can find the same materials used in their story cans outside.

Adaptations for children with special needs

- Some children might have a hard time opening their tin cans; be sure they are easy to open or provide another type of container (e.g., a box that the lid just rests on).

Developmental Range for "Story Can": Supporting Children at Different Levels

Earlier	Middle	Later
Children may	*Children may*	*Children may*
• Use the people figures and tell simple details of a story.	• Tell a story with their materials.	• Add more details to their stories and combine their materials (and stories) with other children's materials (and stories).
• Pretend that the pine cones are trees. Use one-word descriptions to characterize their pretend play (e.g., "woods," "trees," or "lake").	• Pretend with more of their materials, such as the pine cones, sticks, and rocks.	• Pretend with all the materials.
• Pretend with materials but not really tell a story.	• Use descriptive language to talk about their materials (e.g., "dark woods," "cool lake," or "tall trees").	• Use descriptive language ("dark, scary forest"; "tall pine trees"; and/or "cold, blue lake").
Adults can	*Adults can*	*Adults can*
• Listen to what children say, repeating some of their words. For example, after a child says, "I am walking through the trees," respond by saying "Once upon a time there was a boy walking through the trees."	• Listen to the children's story, look for a natural opening, and then join their story using their materials.	• Listen for descriptive vocabulary that is related to the children's story (e.g., if a child tells a story about finding a monster in the woods, she might say words such as "horns," "claws," and "Cyclops").
• Ask "I wonder what your person will do next?"	• Role-play with children, adding descriptive words to their play (e.g., if a child says, "The girl was walking through the dark woods," say something like "These woods are really dark and cold").	• Join the children's play when there is a natural opening and add some more complex details to children's stories.
	• Use other descriptive words to describe what children are doing (e.g., "She is scared; she's frightened of the dark forest"). Ask the children how they think the character is feeling throughout their story.	

Falling Leaves

Children use a parachute to make leaves from trees "fly" and fall down.

Time of day

Large-group time

Content areas

- Physical Development and Health
- Science and Technology

Materials

For each child and teacher:

- Variety of leaves (this activity is ideal for the fall season)

Shared materials:

- Large parachute

Backup materials:

- None

Beginning

- Introduce the activity by talking with children about leaves falling from the trees.
- Pass out leaves for the children to look at while you talk.
- Ask the children if they have seen any leaves on the ground. Have a conversation about what they have seen happening to leaves outside.
- Ask the children why they think the leaves are falling at this time.

Middle

- Tell the children that you need their help to make leaves fall in the classroom.
- Spread out the parachute, and have children place their leaves on top of it.
- Shake the parachute so that the leaves fly into the air and fall back down.
- Alternate between moving the parachute fast and slow.

End

- Lay the parachute on the floor, and ask the children to sit on the edge of it. Remind them that they can look for leaves at outside time.
- Transition the children to the next part of the daily routine by the color they are sitting on (e.g., "If you are sitting on blue, please go get your coat on for outside time" and so forth, until all the children have transitioned).

Ideas for follow-up

- Add leaves to your art area.

- Take the parachute outside and play with it with the leaves children find.

Adaptations for children with special needs

- Some children have a hard time holding on to a parachute. Sew in loops (if they are not already there) that children can put around their wrist to shake the parachute.

Children love to jump in the fall leaves! After making a big pile of the leaves (with the help of the children), this teacher brought some leaves into her class for the large-group time with the parachute and then also added leaves to the art area.

Story Stones

Children draw pictures on stones to pretend with during their play.

Time of day

Small-group time

Content areas

- Language, Literacy, and Communication
- Creative Arts

Materials

For each child and teacher:

- Markers
- 5 to 8 stones
- Basket to hold above materials

Shared materials:

- None

Backup materials:

- None

Beginning

- Start with a simple, made-up story with some stones that you have already drawn on (it is best to draw simple stick figures and shapes for the setting). Think of a story that is related to the play happening in your classroom so that children are interested. For example, if children have been playing out vacations, start with some stones on which you have drawn an airplane (long oval with rounded triangles for the wings); a Mom, Dad, and child (stick figures); and a simple suitcase (rectangle).

- Begin your story by showing the children the Mom and Dad talking to each other, and say something like "Today is our vacation. We should go wake up Tony so he can pack his bag. We don't want to be late for the airplane." Have the Mom and Dad "walk" over to Tony and wake him up so he can pack his suitcase and go with his family to the airplane. Then say to the children "What do you think could happen next in my story? I have a blank stone to draw on." Listen to the children's ideas, and draw the next part.

- Tell the children that they are going to make their own story stones. Talk with the children about whom and what they could draw, reminding them of favorite stories they know and the people in those stories.

Middle

- Pass out the baskets of materials to the children.

- Walk around the table to kneel down with each child, noticing what he or she is drawing on the stones.

- Talk with each child about his or her character and setting ideas.

End

- Let the children know that the activity will be ending in three minutes.

- Tell the children that you are going to collect their stones to be used for the next day and ask them to leave them at their seats. (Be sure to write the children's names on the backs of their stones so that you can return them the next day.)

- Tell the children a story to move to the next part of the daily routine. For example, you might say, "Once there were eight children who cleaned up their markers and stones. Then these children stood up, pushed in their chairs, and walked over to the sink to wash their hands."

Ideas for follow-up

- Use the story stones (yours and the children's) the next day for small-group time. Instead of using just the stones for pretend play, add small people figures to the stones to see what stories children create.

- Add the story stones to the book area for children to tell stories with.

Adaptations for children with special needs

- Include larger rocks for those children who might have a hard time drawing on small ones.

Developmental Range for "Story Stones": Supporting Children at Different Levels

Earlier	Middle	Later
Children may	*Children may*	*Children may*
• Scribble on their stones. • Notice that their scribble looks like something. • Copy the same characters and settings an adult used as an example.	• Draw a simple character or setting (e.g., a square and triangle for a house, a circle for a head of a girl). • Identify characters of stories that are familiar to them.	• Draw characters and settings with details (e.g., a person with a body and head, a house with a door and a window). • Think of more detailed objects to draw, such as a pet in the story or a car the characters use.
Adults can	*Adults can*	*Adults can*
• Scribble on their own stones while sitting next to children. • Say what their stone looks like (e.g., "Mine looks like a boy"). • Remind children of stories that they know and like. Ask "I wonder who you could draw out of that story?"	• Acknowledge children's work (e.g., "I see the girl's head"). • Talk with children about the story that they remember. • Remind children of other settings, characters, or stories that they like. • Ask children about a particular book to spark their memory.	• Acknowledge children's work and converse with them about the story they are thinking of. • Have children tell the story aloud, which might remind them of something else in the story. • Work with children to remember the details of the characters and setting (e.g., "I remember that boy had a hat on his head").

Nature Patterns

Children make patterns with natural materials.

Time of day

Small-group time

Content areas

- Mathematics
- Creative Arts

Materials

For each child and teacher:

- Variety of natural materials (e.g., twigs, leaves, pine cones, seashells, stones)
- *(Optional)* 8 × 10 piece of cardboard
- *(Optional)* Glue
- Basket to hold above materials

Shared materials:

- Pictures of patterns that occur naturally in the environment
- Baskets to sort materials (for cleanup)

Backup materials:

- Camera

Beginning

- Show children pictures of natural patterns. Talk with them about what they see and explain what the pictures are of.
- Use the word *pattern* when talking to children about the pictures.
- Tell the children that they can make their own nature patterns using the materials in their baskets.
- Pass out the baskets to children so they can explore their materials. Spread the photos that you have collected around the table.

Middle

- Talk with the children about what they are doing and the patterns they are working on. For example, you might say, "I see that you are putting your twigs in a row."
- Offer the photos you have collected as ideas that children can look at when making their patterns.
- *(Optional)* Take, or allow children to take, photos of their nature patterns.
- *(Optional)* Suggest that children glue their patterns down on their piece of cardboard.

End

- Let the children know that the activity will be ending in five minutes.

- Have the children sort their materials into baskets in the middle of the table and/or set the cardboard pieces somewhere to dry (if children glued the materials on them).

- Remind the children that you will add these materials to the toy area or art area, and ask them to hop to the next part of the routine.

Ideas for follow-up

- Make a classroom book with nature pattern pictures.

- Print children's pictures and add them to your book as well.

- Add photos of natural patterns to walls in your classroom's art area.

Adaptations for children with special needs

- Some children seem to be overwhelmed with too many choices of materials. For these children, offer them only two types of natural materials.

> **Bright Idea**
> **Pictures of Patterns**
>
> To find pictures of patterns that occur naturally in the environment, look on the Internet or in library books (e.g., *Alphabet City* by Stephen T. Johnson or *Andy Goldsworthy: A Collaboration With Nature* by Andy Goldsworthy). Alternatively, take pictures of natural patterns you have created beforehand.

This child uses shells (and a feather) to make a pattern and then glues his pattern on a piece of cardboard.

Developmental Range for "Nature Patterns": Supporting Children at Different Levels

Earlier	Middle	Later
Children may	*Children may*	*Children may*
• Pile their materials on top of the table. • Sort their materials into piles.	• Create a simple pattern or design with their materials. • Try to copy a pattern in a picture but not be able to figure it all out.	• Create a more complex pattern (e.g., AABBCC-AABBCC). • Explain in detail how or why their design is a pattern. • Create more of a design pattern (not necessarily in a line), such as a circle made out of twigs or a maze created from stones.
Adults can	*Adults can*	*Adults can*
• Support children by commenting on what they see (e.g., "I see you have your leaves, twigs, and rocks all in a pile"). • Encourage children to talk about their patterns by saying something like "Tell me about your pattern." • Remind children that a lot of patterns are in a straight line and help children create these simple patterns.	• Talk with children about their patterns, encouraging them to describe what they have made. • Help children slow down and look at each part of the picture to better see the elements of the pattern. • Encourage children to use the materials provided to make their own variation of the pattern shown in pictures. For example, you might say, "We don't have big trees to use, but how can you use these sticks instead?"	• Comment on what they see children doing (e.g., "I see you are putting your stones in a swirly shape"). • Encourage children to explain their patterns. Say, for example, "Tell me about your pattern. I see it looks like this picture."

4
Recycled and Scrap Materials

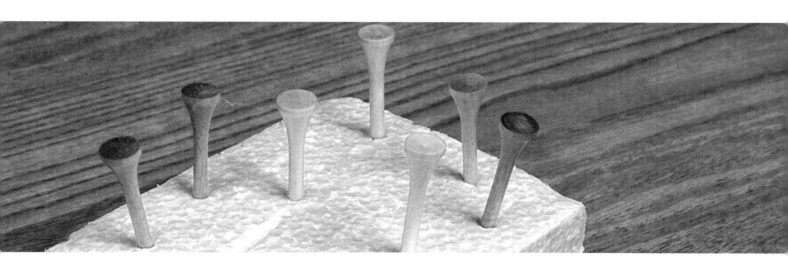

What Are Recycled and Scrap Materials?

While using a variety of recycled plastic milk and juice caps at small-group time, Macy sorts her basket full of caps into three piles: blue, yellow, and white. As Spencer makes a pattern with his caps, he touches each one and says, "Red, white, red, white, red, white." Riley tries stacking her caps in a tower. "They are tricky," she says, "because they keep falling over." Olivia spreads her caps on the table and uses her fingers to "walk on them."

Recycled and scrap materials are items you use every day and put in your trash can or recycle bin, such as paper towel tubes, empty food boxes, bottle caps, and plastic bottles. These are materials that can be used as they are for pretend play or a different purpose, or, with a little creativity, turned into something else.

Like all the materials described in this book, recycled and scrap materials are open ended and free or inexpensive. In addition, adding these materials to your classroom allows children to experience what recycling means in a concrete way. Although many classrooms have recycling boxes that the teachers and children toss paper into, these recycling boxes don't really help children understand what recycling is. Using recycled and scrap materials in the classroom is one way to expand this understanding.

This child creates a pattern with recycled milk caps.

Where Do I Add Recycled and Scrap Materials in My Classroom?

Recycled and scrap materials, like any material in a preschool classroom, should be stored with similar items (e.g., bottle caps should be stored together in a box or container). When collecting recycled and scrap materials, wash them thoroughly before adding them to the classroom. Be aware of children's allergies — do not use peanut-butter containers if there are children in your classroom who have a peanut or nut allergy (even if the containers have been washed). Finally, do not use containers that may have held harmful or hazardous materials, such as bleach or other strong cleaning solutions.

Below are some examples of recycled and scrap materials and the areas in your classroom where you might find them. Some of the materials listed here are in more than one area, such as corks in the house area and sand and water area. You can provide a material in more than one place or simply rotate the material into different areas. Also listed here are other unconventional ways you might use these materials.

In the House Area
- Yogurt cups (for pretend play)
- Fabric (for scarves)
- Plastic bottles (for pretend play)
- Empty food containers
- Plastic baby food containers with lids
- Corks (for pretend play)
- Buttons collected from old clothing (for pretend play)
- Laundry detergent bottles (for pretend play)

In the Block Area
- Boxes (to make community blocks; see p. 154)
- Paper towel tubes (to use for bowling)
- Plastic bottles (as bowling bottles; see p. 158)

In the Toy Area
- Golf tees (to sort, line up, and count)
- Caps (from milk and juice containers; to sort and count)
- Buttons collected from old clothing (to sort and count)

In the Art Area

- Yogurt cups (for holding crayons)

- Applesauce containers (as paint cups)

- Tennis ball containers (to hold yarn)

- Fabric (for cutting and pasting on paper)

- Boxes (for many different art purposes, including painting, building with, and decorating)

- Caps (from milk and juice containers)

- Paper towel tubes

- Buttons collected from old clothing (for gluing and stringing)

In the Sand and Water Area

- Plastic strainers from microwavable lunches

- Tubes

- Buckets

- Plastic bottles (for dumping and filling)

- Corks (lots of fun in the water!)

In the Woodworking Area

- Golf tees (to push into Styrofoam)

- Styrofoam

In the Outside Play Space

- Tires

- Milk crates (for storage of outside toys)

- Plastic bags (made into jump ropes; see p. 120)

- Large cardboard tubes

Materials for Teachers to Use in Unconventional Ways

- Plastic bottles (to make I spy bottles, sensory bottles, sand timers, and bowling bottles; see pp. 153, 155, 157, and 158)

- Plastic bags (to make plastic bag shakers and jump ropes; see p. 118 and p. 120)

- Paper towel tubes (to make shakers; see p. 118 and p. 156)

- Tin cans (to store materials in for small-group times or to use as story cans; see p. 48)

- Laundry detergent bottles (to make guitars from; see p. 122)

Recycled and Scrap Materials in Classroom Areas

Empty food containers in the house area

Buttons in the toy area

Tennis ball containers (to hold yarn) in the art area

Large cardboard tubes in the outside play space

Where Do I Find Recycled and Scrap Materials?

To find recycled and scrap materials, put on your green hat and be on the look-out everywhere — your home, your school, and local recycling centers and stores — for materials that you would like to add to the classroom. Making a list of materials that you are collecting and asking children's and co-workers' families to collect and bring them in is a great way to get a lot of neat items quickly. Most people really enjoy helping find materials for the classroom, and this is a way they can do so that does not cost money. One teacher had her "aha" moment during a lunch break:

One day, while eating her microwavable lunch, Karen, a teacher, realized that the plastic container her lunch came in could make a great bowl for the children to mix paint in. Then she thought about the strainer part of her lunch container (this was a lunch that steamed in the microwave) and how this could be used. She decided that she would collect more of these strainers and place them in the water table. Karen placed a box inside the lunchroom and sent out an e-mail to her co-workers, asking

One teacher collected 10 sets of these microwavable containers in just one week by asking her colleagues to save them from their lunches.

them to place their washed microwavable lunch containers in the box. By the end of the week, Karen had 10 sets of the containers and strainers to use in her classroom.

Setting up reuse and recycle boxes in the classroom is another way to collect materials you want to use or recycle those you don't want to save. Talk with the children about what materials they can place in the reuse box (e.g., paper towel tubes, food boxes, caps, bottles, boxes) as they finish using these items in the classroom. Adding this reuse box to your classroom also helps children have a better understanding of what recycling means in a very concrete way, as Nigel demonstrates:

After Nigel washes his hands for lunchtime, he uses the last piece of paper towel to dry his hands. He then takes the tube off the dispenser and places it in the classroom's reuse box. "Mary, look! I put a tube in there for the art area!" he says excitedly to his teacher.

In addition, children learn how to take care of the classroom environment by replacing paper towel rolls when they are empty, washing out food containers to reuse them for something else, and sorting the trash and materials to be recycled and reused.

Finally, you might be lucky to have a place in your area that collects recycled and scrap materials for teachers and sells them at low cost (we buy materials from The Scrap Box in Ann Arbor, Michigan). Keeping an open imagination, thinking like a child, and looking at objects with a "new eye" will help you see the treasure within the scraps!

What Can I Do With Recycled and Scrap Materials?

Now that you have collected a lot of treasures, what do you do with them? You can encourage children to use them in new and exciting ways by adding them "as is" to classroom areas, creating new materials from them, and using them in planned ways throughout the daily routine.

Using recycled and scrap materials "as is"

- Store your crayons in yogurt cups, separating the colors into individual cups (this helps children sort the crayons by color and keep them organized). When materials are kept clean and neatly presented, children are more likely to keep them in good condition, as Abby does:

  At cleanup time, Abby picks up the crayons from the pile on the table and names each color as she places them in their corresponding cup.

- Store your golf tees next to Styrofoam. Children enjoy poking the tees into the foam and making different models with the materials.

- Add scrap fabric, bottle caps, boxes, and paper towel tubes to the art area:

  At work time in the art area, Charlie tells Emma, "I'm making my dog a house. This part [points to the fabric] is his bed, and this is where he plays [picks up the tube]." Charlie puts the fabric and tube in an empty box and pretends with his "dog."

- Add milk and juice caps in a basket in the toy area.
- Use empty applesauce cups for paint cups.

  With children's creativity, recycled and scrap materials can become almost anything (see "A Day in the Life of an Open-Ended Material" on pp. 70–71).

Using recycled and scrap materials to create new materials

- Create shakers using paper towel tubes (see p. 118 and p. 156).
- Use plastic bottles and bags to make many different materials (e.g., using plastic bags to make jump ropes):

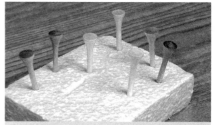

Bright Idea
Styrofoam and Golf Tees

Use Styrofoam and golf tees with children that need more fine-motor practice; they can have lots of fun grasping the golf tees and using their muscles to push them into the Styrofoam. You can also use Styrofoam and golf tees for a planning or recall strategy. Draw area signs on a large piece of Styrofoam, and ask children to push the golf tee into the part of Styrofoam that represents the area where they want to play or already played in. Children then elaborate on what they want to do or already did.

At outside time, Stephen and Molly lay jump ropes end to end in a long line along the sidewalk. "This is the road; don't go over the line!" says Stephen to the other children.

- Find two caps (from juice or milk containers) that fit inside each other to make into small shakers (see p. 75).

- Use tennis ball containers to store yarn in so it won't get tangled. Cut a slit in the lid, drop the yarn in vertically, and pull the yarn through the slit in the lid (see p. 63).

- Cut the large side off of cereal boxes and glue the cardboard to the back of photos to make them sturdier.

- Make "guitars" using rubber bands or plastic stretchy string and an empty laundry bottle (see p. 122):

During work time, Carlos, Tommy, and Drew grab the guitars from the toy area. Then they make a "stage" with blocks from the block area. They put on hats and sunglasses (from the house area) and tell their teacher that they are a band.

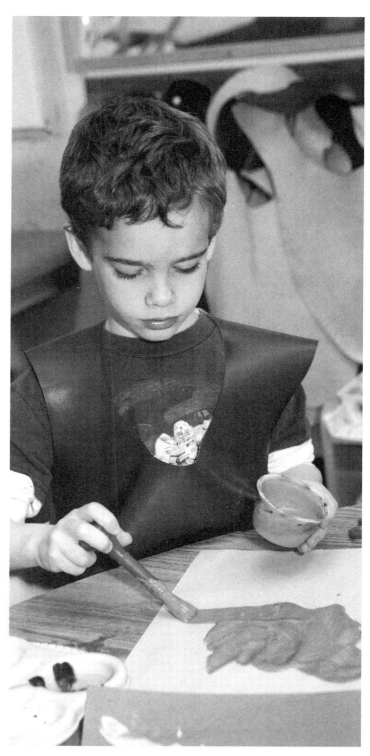

An applesauce container makes a perfect paint cup — small enough so paint isn't wasted but large enough to allow children to mix colors.

Using recycled and scrap materials in the daily routine

- Place tires in your outdoor play space for children to roll around, climb on, or build with:

  While playing outside, Rob and Li stack the tires around themselves and call it their house.

- Use in a planning or recall strategy. For example, draw each classroom area symbol at the bottom of a yogurt cup. At recall time, ask the children to place a marble in the yogurt cup that represents where they worked at work time.

- Use for cleaning time, as shown in the following anecdote:

  Ted, a teacher, passes out the "cleanup buckets" (recycled ice cream tubs) to each child. He says, "Today we have our cleanup buckets to use. Fill your bucket up and then put those toys away."

As with all materials teachers use in the classroom, it is important to play with children in the ways they play with the materials (see "How Do I Use These Materials With Children?" on pp. 20–21 for ideas).

Bright Idea
Sensory Bottles

Look on page 155 for a great idea on how to make sensory bottles using all those water and soda bottles that you have been saving. The glistening water, shiny glitter or sequins, and attractive items in the sensory bottles are very calming to look at and are particularly attractive to children with sensory needs.

Put these bottles in your play refrigerator for children to pretend with in the house area. You can also place them on top of a shelf in a quiet area (such as the book area) or add them to nap baskets for children to use while they are calming down for rest time.

Children find lots of uses for tires in the outside play space.

A Day in the Life of an Open-Ended Material

Hi there! Let me introduce myself. I'm a little yellow, cylinder-shaped sponge. I live on a shelf in the house area in the HighScope Demonstration Preschool in a canister with about 60 other sponges just like me. I lead a very interesting life. In fact, thanks to those active preschoolers, my life is one big adventure. Just this morning, you might say I was very popular with those little humans.

It all started when two little girls mentioned that they were going to use me in their plans. "We're going to have a birthday party," one of them told Sue, their teacher. "Yeah," said the other, "we're going to make cupcakes for the party." Sue inquired, "Cupcakes? Yum! What will you use to make them?" The girls looked over our way, and one said, "The yellow sponges and the pans." So here we go...

Selecting a suit coat, a skirt, and scarves from the collection of dress-up clothing, the girls dressed for the party. Then they came over and took me and my buddies off the shelf. They plopped us into some muffin tins and put us in the play oven. After about 10 seconds, we were pronounced "done." Over to the table we went, where we were served to several partygoers who had gathered. Soon, three children pretending to be puppies joined the party. Down into the dog dish I went. Apparently, in the preschool, puppies enjoy cupcakes too!

After the puppies pretended to eat us, they crawled over to the block area, where several block builders had constructed a large train using the hollow blocks. The puppies sniffed around the train for a bit and then helped to add features to the train. One puppy went to the book area and brought back a large, soft pillow so he would have a comfortable place to rest. Another puppy got some of those same scarves that the birthday party girls were wearing and added those to the train for blankets. The last puppy came over and got the dog dish, with us sponges still sitting inside, and slid us into one of the hollow blocks. (You never know when you might get hungry on a long train ride!) While the block builders put the final touches on their train, two other children were also in the block area using the small unit blocks and little people figures. They were using the blocks for furniture for their free-form house. One child spotted us sponges peeking out from where we had been placed by the puppy. He came over and scooped a handful of us out of the dog dish and brought us over to the unit blocks. "Look," he said, "these could be their beds." He placed each one of us on a square block and carefully placed a figure on each of us. "Shhhh," his playmate said, "they're all sleeping now."

While this was happening, I noticed that some of my pals who had remained in the canister were now being brought over by one of the younger children. She dumped the canister over and began stacking these sponges. First she stacked them up and knocked them over, laughing when they tumbled and fell. She did this several times, each time stacking the sponges a little higher. Then she went to the toy area and brought back the bin of small cars. She stacked up the sponges again, this time using a car to knock them over.

The children who were using us as beds decided to wake up their figures. Then they took some of the figures to the water table for a swim. The boy came back to the block area and picked me up, along with a few of my friends. Now both children were using us to scrub the figures. "Hey," the girl said, "it's a boat!" She had balanced a figure on me again, and together we bobbed on top of the water. The children soon made a game of seeing how many boats (a sponge with a figure balanced on top) they could get floating at once. "One, two, three, four, five, six!" the girl counted. "No, one fell," said the boy, "One, two, three, four, five." "Let's make them all fall," the girl giggled. "Yeah, let's make them all fall," the boy agreed. Together, they splashed and made waves in the water table until all of us sponges were bobbing and all the people figures were sinking slowly to the bottom.

Next, someone came by and announced it was five minutes until cleanup time. Whew! This usually means a break for us. When those five minutes went by, we were scooped out of the water and squeezed — hard — to get the water out of us. At the teacher's suggestion, the children placed us on a paper towel on the counter so we could dry out. From this vantage point, I noticed that some of my colleagues were now being tossed one at a time, back into the canister as if they were basketballs.

The children at the table by me sang a song about recall time. Before I could properly dry out, one of those two little birthday party girls grabbed me and put me in something called a recall bag. She brought me back to her group, took me out of the bag, and shared how she used me to make cupcakes for the party. Then I was returned to the counter so I could finish air drying. I stayed there for the remainder of the morning. At the end of the morning, the children left and the two teachers sat down to chat. I heard them talking about us sponges and learned that tomorrow they're going to use us with the parachute to play a game with the children called "Popcorn." I'm not sure what that is, but I think I'll be in for quite a time tomorrow!

— Adapted from "A Day in the Life of an Open-Ended Material," *HighScope Extensions* 22(3) (Marshall, 2008, p. 3).

Activities for Recycled and Scrap Materials

Making Shakers

Children use recycled caps from bottles to make musical instruments.

Time of day

Small-group time

Content areas

- Science and Technology

Materials

For each child and teacher:

- A pair of different-sized plastic caps that fit inside one another
- Rice in a paper cup
- Dried beans in a paper cup
- Basket to hold the above materials

Shared materials:

- Masking or packing tape
- Permanent marker

Backup materials:

- None

Beginning

- Talk to the children about the different shakers they have used in the classroom. Ask them if they think all shakers make the same noise, and discuss loud and soft noises.

- Show the children two caps that you found that fit inside one another, and tell them that you (and they) will be exploring the different sounds with the materials in their baskets.

- Add dried beans to your caps, and ask children if they think the sound will be loud or soft. Shake your shaker and see what sound it makes. Say "I wonder what would happen if I placed the rice in these caps instead." (You don't have to actually do this step; just get children interested in it!)

- Pass out the baskets with the materials, and let the children get started.

Middle

- As children try out different materials, encourage them to predict what sound they think a particular material will make when they shake their caps.

- Listen to children's predictions and their results. Encourage children to share their thinking about their predictions and results.

End

- Give children a signal that the activity will be ending at a given time (e.g., two minutes).

- Tell children to choose the material(s) they want to keep inside their caps. Once they have chosen their materials, help them tape their shakers closed and write their names on their shakers with a permanent marker.

- Transition to the next part of the daily routine by having the children shake their bodies (e.g., say "Let's shake our bodies to snacktime").

Ideas for follow-up

- Use the shakers during a large-group time with music or for a "marching band," where children march around the room.

- Add the shakers to the other musical instruments in the classroom.

You can make a collection of shakers from different types of caps and recycled containers and rice or beans.

Developmental Range for "Making Shakers": Supporting Children at Different Levels

Earlier	Middle	Later
Children may	*Children may*	*Children may*
• Put the materials in the caps and shake them without making any predictions.	• Make predictions about the different sounds the shakers will make and may be incorrect about their predictions.	• Choose the rice or beans with an idea of how each material will sound.
• Use one or two words to describe the sound they are hearing (e.g., "This one is loud" or "This is soft and quiet").	• Experiment with the materials to find the sound that they want.	• Make accurate predictions about how the materials will sound in their shakers.
	• Describe the sounds in more detail and compare them.	• Explain why a certain material makes a certain sound.
		• Compare the sounds of the two materials in the shakers and describe them in more detail.
Adults can	*Adults can*	*Adults can*
• Talk with children as they use the materials, describing what they are doing and encouraging them to make predictions (e.g., "I wonder if those beans are going to make a loud or soft noise").	• Repeat the children's comparisons of sounds (e.g., say "This one is loud and this one is soft"), and inquire about why they think this is.	• Encourage the children to explain their findings about the different sounds and the different materials.
• Comment in more detail about the sound once children describe the sound they are hearing (e.g., "That soft sound reminds me of rain").	• Talk with children about their predictions and ideas of sounds.	• Ask the children what might happen if they were to add more or less of one material in the shaker. Ask, for example, "I wonder what would happen if you only put three beans inside the caps?"

Patterns With Buttons

Children use recycled buttons to make patterns.

Time of day

Small-group time

Content areas

- Mathematics

Materials

For each child and teacher:

- At least 8 or more buttons with one attribute (color, size, shape) in common and two different attributes
- Small container to hold above materials

Shared materials:

- None

Backup materials:

- A third type of button with another attribute (e.g., round buttons in another color)

Beginning

- Start by using your own set of buttons and lay them out in a scattered arrangement on the table in front of you.

- Ask the children what they notice about the buttons. Listen to their ideas, and talk with the children about the similarities and differences of the buttons.

- Once children have identified the attributes you were planning on (e.g., they recognize that the buttons all are round but that some are red and some are blue), tell them that you are going to make a pattern with your buttons.

- Arrange the buttons in an ABABAB pattern, naming the relevant attribute each time you place a button down; for example, "Red, blue, red, blue, red, blue." (To establish a pattern, each item must be repeated at least three times. Therefore, always provide at least three repetitions when talking about a pattern with a child.)

- Tell the children that you have some buttons that they can use to make their own patterns, and then pass out the materials. (Each child should have a set of buttons with one attribute in common and two different attributes, e.g., one child might have eight round buttons, some of which are red, while the rest are blue; another child might have all purple buttons that are circles and squares.)

Middle

- As children work with the buttons, name and talk to them about the different properties of the buttons.
- Point to and recite the order of the buttons in their patterns; for example, you might say, "Square, circle, square, circle, square, circle."
- Copy children's patterns with your own materials.
- Start a pattern with your own materials, and ask children to help you complete it.
- Offer the backup buttons to children who have quickly made their ABABAB pattern. Talk with them about the different properties of buttons and how to make an ABCABCABC pattern.

End

- After giving the children a three-minute warning that the activity will be ending soon, ask them to put their buttons into baskets.
- Remind the children that they can use the buttons the next day at work time.
- Have the children transition to the next part of the daily routine with a movement pattern (e.g., jump, clap, jump, clap, jump, clap or hop, step, hop, step, hop, step).

Ideas for follow-up

- Place the buttons in the toy area, and tell children about them the next day on your message board.
- Use other recycled materials, such as caps from milk and juice containers, to make patterns.

Developmental Range for "Patterns With Buttons": Supporting Children at Different Levels

Earlier	Middle	Later
Children may	*Children may*	*Children may*
• Sort their buttons into piles.	• Create a simple pattern with their buttons.	• Create a more complex pattern (e.g., AABAAB-AAB or ABCABCABC).
• State a difference or similarity about their buttons.	• Name their pattern and explain why it is a pattern.	• Help other children create patterns.
• Line up their buttons in no particular order.		
Adults can	*Adults can*	*Adults can*
• Comment on what they see children doing with their buttons.	• Copy a child's pattern with their materials.	• Talk with children about their materials' properties (e.g., describe the colors, shapes, or number of holes in the buttons).
• Point out the properties of the buttons that children are using or touching.	• Encourage children to talk about their pattern.	• Offer children another set of buttons that has another property or attribute, converse with them about what they notice about these new materials, and challenge them to make a new pattern using all of their buttons.
• Create their own pattern and offer children to copy or help finish it.	• Challenge children to create a more complex pattern by making one and asking them to help complete it.	

Drumming on Our Buckets

Children use recycled buckets as drums.

Time of day

Large-group time

Content areas

- Creative Arts
- Physical Development and Health

Materials

For each child and teacher:

- Recycled bucket (e.g., a plastic ice cream tub, a large sour cream tub)

Beginning

- As children sit down in your large-group space, tell them to pretend their hands are drumsticks. Ask them what it would look like if they were drumming on a drum.

- Pass out the buckets to children, and let them explore different ways to pat them.

- Teach the children a new song (to the tune of "Here We Go Round the Mulberry Bush"):

> This is how I pat my drum, pat my drum, pat my drum
>
> This is how I pat my drum during large group.

(Repeat stanza.)

Middle

- Start by patting the drum with your hands, and sing the song.

- Ask children for their ideas on how to pat their drums. Try out each idea while singing the song, and add children's names into the song, as in this example:

> This is how Emily pats, Emily pats, Emily pats
>
> This is how Emily pats at large group.

End

- When large group is close to ending, tell the children that they can pat their drum however they want while you (and the children) sing:

  This is how we pat our drums, pat our drums, pat our drums

  This is how we pat our drums before we put them away.

- Ask the children to stack their drums on top of each other.

- Sing the song again while moving to the next part of the day, for example:

  This is how we walk to lunch, walk to lunch, walk to lunch

  This is how we walk to lunch after large group.

Ideas for follow-up

- Add this song to your songbook, and use it with or without the drums.

- Add buckets to your classroom with the other musical instruments.

After patting her bucket to show children how to use their hands as drumsticks, this teacher asks the children to share their ideas on how to pat their "drum."

Creating a Home

Children use a variety of recycled materials to construct a home.

Time of day

Small-group time

Content areas

- Social and Emotional Development
- Language, Literacy, and Communication
- Creative Arts

Materials

For each child and teacher:

- Medium-sized box
- Fabric scraps
- Buttons
- Caps (from milk and juice containers)
- Glue
- Basket to hold smaller materials

Shared materials:

- Markers

Backup materials:

- Extra boxes
- Scissors

Beginning

- Start the activity by engaging the children in a conversation about their homes, what type of home they live in (e.g., apartment, house), what their home looks like, and all the parts of a home (e.g., door, roof). Be sure to bring out the similarities and differences in where children live.

- Tell children that today they can make their own home, and show them a box and the supporting materials. Point out the markers in the middle of the table.

Middle

- Hand out the materials to children, and encourage them to explore them. (Be open to children who are not interested in making a home but are interested in exploring the materials in other ways.)

- Visit each child, conversing about what he or she knows about homes and what he or she is adding to the house.

- Help children figure out how to make the different parts of their homes using the given materials.

End

- Tell the children that the activity will be ending in five minutes.

- After five minutes, ask the children to place all their extra materials into their baskets and have a designated place that they can put their homes.

- Tell the children that they can finish their homes (if needed) at work time, or they can take them home.

Ideas for follow-up

- Place the recycled materials, including boxes, in the art area.

- Place some of the homes (the ones children wanted to keep at school) in the block or toy area for children to use with people figures.

This teacher found a creative use for a very large-sized box — a comfy reading nook to share a story.

Developmental Range for "Creating a Home": Supporting Children at Different Levels

Earlier	Middle	Later
Children may	*Children may*	*Children may*
• Glue items on their box without mentioning a home or house.	• Explain what their homes look like in short sentences (e.g., "Mine has fabric"), adding more details about the parts of their homes.	• Choose materials intentionally and use them as they intended (e.g., choose a button, say "This is going to be a window," and then glue it on their home).
• Talk about their homes in one or two words; for example, they may say "buttons" while pointing to them.	• Glue items on their home and then state what the material looks like.	• Have a clear image in their minds of what their own homes look like.
• Glue many items on their home without identifying what the pieces are intended for.	• Add simple parts to their home, such as a door, windows, or chimney.	• Add more details to the different parts of their homes (e.g., a shade to a window, bricks on the siding, etc.).
Adults can	*Adults can*	*Adults can*
• Ask children simple, open-ended questions to help them think about their homes and what they look like.	• Converse with children about what they are doing.	• Comment on the different details they see children making in their homes.
• Comment on what children are doing with their recycled materials.	• Copy children's ideas on their own home.	• Talk with children about the homes they live in and converse about similarities and differences in their home and other homes.
	• Talk with children about more details they could add to the parts they already have on their homes (e.g., "I see you have a door, but how do you open the door?").	

5

Low-Cost Materials

What Are Low-Cost Materials?

Sam carries a length of drainage tubing up in the climber with him. He drops one end down off the side of the climber and puts the other end to his mouth. Through one end of the tubing he yells, "Hello down there." "Hello, Sam," replies a teacher through the other end of the tubing. "I need help. My house [climber] is on fire," says Sam. "Oh no! Let me call the fire department," replies the teacher. The teacher then gathers some children together to help save Sam and tells Sam (through the tubing), "Sam, the fire department is on their way." The children rush up into the climber and help Sam down.

Low-cost materials are inexpensive items you purchase that children use in the classroom as is (e.g., craft sticks, PVC pipe, hair curlers), as Ann Marie demonstrates with another way to use drainage tubing:

Ann Marie pulls a length of drainage tubing to the top of the hill on the playground. She then brings some small balls to the top of the hill. She puts one ball after another down the tubing until they are all down the hill. Then she runs to collect the balls and does this all over again.

These children (and their teacher) use the drainage tube as a telephone to talk to each other on the playground.

Children use low-cost materials in many different ways to suit their play (such as drainage tubing in the two previous anecdotes). You can also turn low-cost materials into other objects or toys children can use in the classroom. For example, you can buy inexpensive sponges and make them into sponge balls or purchase ribbons and create ribbon wands. In addition, low-cost materials can supply a classroom set of objects or toys. Instead of having just a few balls or shakers for the entire class to share, you can make a classroom set of balls or shakers with these inexpensive materials.

Where Do I Add Low-Cost Materials in My Classroom?

Like any materials in a preschool classroom, low-cost materials should be stored with similar items (e.g., place store-bought silverware next to the plates and cups in the house area; add clothespin people [see p. 93] in a basket by the other figures in your classroom).

On the following page are some examples of low-cost materials and the areas in your classroom you might find them. Some of the materials listed there are in more than one area, such as PVC piping in the sand and water area, the block area, and the outside play space. You can provide a material in more than one place or simply rotate the material into different areas, depending on the play happening there.

A cookie sheet can be used as a magnet story board. This teacher created her own magnets from pictures of the children in her class and added them to the cookie sheet.

In the House Area

- Silverware
- Clothespins
- Colored noodles (see p. 130)
- Beans
- Ice cube trays
- Metal cookie sheets

In the Art Area

- Craft sticks
- Felt sheets
- Paper plates

In the Sand and Water Area

- PVC piping
- Pulleys
- Sponges

In the Toy Area

- Bendy hair rollers
- Ice cube trays
- Clothespin people (see p. 93)

In the Woodworking Area

- Golf tees
- Wood scraps
- Nails

In the Block Area

- Sponge balls (see p. 116)
- PVC piping

In the Outside Play Space

- Drainage tubing
- PVC piping
- Stretchy bands
- Pulleys
- Buckets

Materials for Teachers to Use in Unconventional Ways

- Super glue (used by teachers to make other materials or glue things permanently shut, such as sensory bottles)
- Rice (to make shakers; see p. 74 and p. 159)
- Beans (to make shakers and bean-bags; see p. 74 and p. 154)
- Socks (to make beanbags; see p. 154)
- Sponges (to make sponge balls; see p. 116)
- Cookie sheets (to make magnet story boards; see p. 152)
- Noodles (to make colored noodles; see p. 130)

Low-Cost Materials in Classroom Areas

PVC piping in the sand and water area

Bendy hair rollers in the toy area

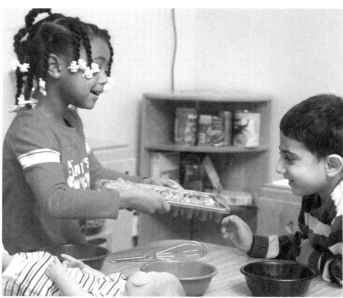

Ice cube trays in the house area

Where Do I Find Low-Cost Materials?

Finding low-cost materials takes some thought and practice. To find the best deals, put on your bargain shopping hat and always be on the lookout for materials on sale. Many stores (such as your local superstore) have low-cost, dollar, or clearance aisles. (I know that I cannot walk into a superstore without checking out the dollar section!) Dollar stores also have great finds (see pp. 92–93). Stores usually have a set time of the month when they receive new merchandise and clearance out older items. Ask your local store manager when the store puts items on clearance, and plan your shopping during its clearance days. Resale shops and garage sales are also great places to look around and bargain. For items such as drainage tubing, PVC piping, and pulleys, visit your local hardware or home improvement store.

The teachers in this classroom drilled holes in a piece of wood that they placed over the sand and water table and then added PVC piping to enhance children's play in this area.

What Can I Do With Low-Cost Materials?

Here are some ideas for using low-cost materials both inside your classroom and in your outdoor play area, and during various parts of your classroom routine.

Inside your classroom

- Place low-cost materials in baskets in different areas of the classroom, and let the children make their own decisions about how to use them. For a material with a particular use, such as clothespin people, add that item to the area where children would usually find small figures. In David's preschool classroom, the teacher added the colored noodles to the house area:

  At work time in the house area, David pours colored noodles on a cookie sheet and puts them in the play stove. "I'm making mac and cheese like my grandpa does," he says.

- Add or affix PVC piping to your sand and water table, which adds to the possibilities of the table and enhances the play happening there as Tanner demonstrates:

  Tanner pours a cupful of sand down the PVC funnel and pipe and says, "Watch, if I do a lot [of sand], it takes a long time to go down [the funnel]."

As part of your classroom routine

- Collect stretchy knit fabric or old bathing suit fabric from your own collection or a fabric store, cut the fabric into long pieces, and loop the ends with a knot. Use these stretchy bands for large-group times — children love to put them on their feet and stretch them or use them with their hands.

- Introduce bendy hair rollers (the kind that can be straightened all the way out) at a small-group time so children can bend and twist them into letters and shapes (see "Hair Curler Letters" on p. 98 for a small-group activity). Then add them to your toy area.

Twenty Dollars for Classroom Materials... How Far Can It Go?

When presenting my first workshop about homemade and low-cost materials, I wanted to challenge myself to find out what (and how many) materials I could get if I pushed myself to think outside the box. So I headed to my nearest dollar store with $20 in hand. (With only this much money in my pocket, I figured it would be all I could spend.)

Colored noodles made from noodles, food coloring, and rubbing alcohol

I started my challenge by thinking about the classroom teachers who have a very limited budget year to year and have to provide materials for 20 or more children. I then began to think about those children and the experiences I would want them to have in my classroom. I wanted materials that would be of interest to my children that they could use in different ways.

As I entered this haven of low-cost materials (aka the dollar store), I saw that it had a wide variety of items, from toiletries and food to holiday decorations and small tools. I also quickly realized

that finding materials would nevertheless be a challenge. The aisle labeled "Toys" seemed like an obvious place to start. There I found indoor toys, outdoor toys, some toys targeted specifically for boys and girls, and some items whose purpose I couldn't figure out. Some of the toys were interesting, items that I would have actually considered buying for my classroom, such as toy dinosaurs. But I would have had to buy 10 packages of dinosaurs to have enough for a classroom set, and then I'd only have $10 left. I decided to keep looking.

I came across a teacher section in the store, which had brightly colored, attractive-looking cutouts of objects. I stared at these for a while, not sure what I would do with these cutouts. I knew I was not wasting my $20 here, so I moved on.

Finally, I got to the arts and crafts section; I expected to find tons of things there. I looked carefully at all the items and

Sponge balls made from sponges and string

selected craft sticks, super glue, felt sheets, and clothespins. It was not a ton of items, but I knew I could use these in some way.

After the disappointing arts and craft aisle (this aisle was supposed to be for making things, I thought), I found the jackpot — the kitchen section! Here I picked up beans, rice, pasta, sponges, ice cube trays, food coloring, and metal cookie sheets. I knew these items could be used in many different ways or could be made into other materials. I also found socks, rubbing alcohol, paper plates, and resealable plastic bags. I looked around the store

Clothespin people made from clothespins, pipe cleaners, and markers

some more and could not decide on anything else to buy, so I headed to the checkout counter. The moment of truth… drum roll, please! My grand total was $13.66, which made me super excited. Outsiders might think, "Big deal. She didn't buy anything that can be used for classroom sets of toys." But they would be wrong. From these items, I made

- A classroom set of sponge balls (since I bought two packages of 10 sponges)

- Shakers (from the beans and rice and recycled materials I had in the classroom)

- Magnet boards (from the metal cookie sheets)

- Clothespin people

- Beanbags (from the socks and beans)

- Colored noodles (from the noodles, food coloring, and rubbing alcohol) that children could sort into ice cube trays

- Felt story boards (from the felt sheets; some I cut into shapes and others I glued onto cardboard for the felt boards)

- Craft sticks and some paper plates for the art area

- Paper plates for catching and tossing sponge balls at large-group time

But I would have to make another trip to the dollar store to spend the $6.40 remaining from my $20 (by buying five more metal cookie sheets to put into the classroom and two more double packs of ice cube trays for sorting). I still needed to spend money on some materials that could not be found in a dollar store, such as Legos and high-quality paint. But, with a little creativity and just a little money, I found out that I could make a lot of things for my classroom!

In your outdoor play area

- Add pulleys to your playground equipment. Affix a bucket on one end of a rope, thread the pulley, and loop the other end of the rope to make a handle for children to pull on:

  At outside time Melissa is on top of the tree house. She calls down to Robin, a teacher, and says, "Bring up the baby." Robin places the baby doll Melissa had been playing with in the bucket and uses the pulley to deliver it to her. Melissa then yells down, "Hold on. I will feed her and then send her back down to sleep." She pretends to feed the baby doll with some rocks and then places her back in the bucket.

- Place stretchy bands in a tub or container in your outdoor storage space for children to use in their own ways. Stretchy bands are also great for large-motor skills, as noted previously.

Bright Idea
Beanbags at Planning/Recall Times

Use homemade sock beanbags with inexpensive buckets for planning or recall times. Tape classroom area signs on the buckets, and ask the children to drop the beanbag in the bucket with the sign for the area where they want to play or already have played.

As with all materials teachers use in the classroom, it is important to play with children in the ways they play with the materials (see "How Do I Use These Materials With Children?" on pp. 20–21 for ideas). Be sure to look over chapter 6 to find out what other materials you can make with your store-bought supplies.

During outside time, this teacher helps two children create a pulley with a bucket so they can deliver acorns to the tree house.

Activities for Low-Cost Materials

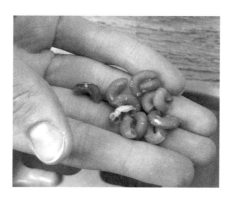

Hair Curler Letters

Children form letters using bendy hair rollers.

Time of day

Small-group time

Content areas

- Language, Literacy, and Communication
- Physical Development and Health

Materials

For each child and teacher:

- 8 to 10 bendy hair curlers of different sizes
- Basket to hold above materials

Shared materials:

- Letter cards

Backup materials:

- Paper and something to write with

Beginning

- Explain to children that you have some materials that bend and twist. Show them your set of hair curlers.

- Tell the children that these are called "letter makers" and that children can bend them into whatever letters they want.

- Bend your curler into a letter to demonstrate how the curlers work.

- Pass out the materials to children, and encourage them to explore the materials.

Middle

- Talk with children about what letters they are making, helping them remember the lines in the letters. For example, you might say, "David, I see that you are making an uppercase *E*. The *E* has a big line and three little lines."

- Once children have explored the curlers for a while, place the letter cards on the table. Tell the children that they can look at these to help remember what the letters look like.

- Ask children to help you make your letter or name.

End

- Give the children a three-minute reminder that the activity will be ending soon.

- Ask the children to place the "letter makers" in one basket and put the letter cards in a pile. Tell them that you will place these "letter makers" in the toy area if they want to use them at work time.

- Transition children to the next part of your daily routine by the letters in their names. For example, you might say, "If your name starts with a *B,* you can go to snacktime" and so forth, until all the children have moved on to the next part of the daily routine.

Ideas for follow-up

- Use the curlers to make shapes or numbers in another small-group time.

- Use other low-cost materials to make letters, such as pipe cleaners or play dough.

Adaptations for children with special needs

- Some children might need some help bending the curlers into letters. Encourage these children to try manipulating the curlers first, and then suggest simple letters for them to make.

A child uses one curler to create a small N *and several curlers to make larger* Ns.

Developmental Range for "Hair Curler Letters": Supporting Children at Different Levels

Earlier	Middle	Later
Children may	*Children may*	*Children may*
• Say some letter names while bending the hair curlers, which may not match the shapes they are making. • Make familiar letters, such as the first one in their name. • Have a difficult time bending the curlers into their desired shape.	• Name many letters and make the sound of the letters they are looking at on the letter cards. • Form some letters out of the curlers.	• Say a word as they make the beginning letter or attempt to make the entire word out of the curlers. • Make additional letters (besides the familiar letters in their names). • Have an easy time bending the letters into a desired shape.
Adults can	*Adults can*	*Adults can*
• Offer children the corresponding letter card to the letter they choose and point out how to make the letter (e.g., "The *A* has two big lines and one little line going across it"). • Encourage children to make more letters that may be familiar to them. • Support children who are having a difficult time bending letters by making specific comments about the shape they did make (e.g., "I see you made a large curve) and then help them problem-solve (e.g., "How could you bend this to make it curved more like the *C* you want?").	• Comment on the letters a child has made (e.g., "I see you made a *D,* an *F,* and an *E*"). • Ask children to make another familiar letter. For example, you might say, "I wonder if you could make my letter. My name starts with the *mmm* sound. It is a letter *M.*"	• Help children sound out the word they are trying to make. • Comment on all the letters children have made with the curlers. • Encourage children to assist peers who have a more difficult time bending the letters.

Sorting Noodles

Children sort colored noodles into ice cube trays.

Time of day

Small-group time

Content areas

- Science and Technology

Materials

For each child and teacher:

- Approximately 20 to 50 noodles in three different colors and shapes; see p. 130 for colored noodle instructions
- Ice cube tray
- Basket or tray to hold above materials

Shared materials:

- Basket for cleanup

Backup materials:

- Colored noodles in different shapes and colors

Beginning

- Make up a story about how all your noodles became disorganized and now you need the children's help to sort them.

- Show the children your noodles, and talk with them about what they notice about the noodles (the different colors and shapes). Note that your set (and the children's set) of noodles should include three different colors and shapes (e.g., blue bowtie, macaroni, and rigatoni noodles; red bowtie, macaroni, and rigatoni noodles; and green bowtie, macaroni, and rigatoni noodles).

- Show the children the ice cube tray, and tell them that you are using it as a sorting tray to help keep all the noodles separated.

- Pass out the materials to the children, and say "I wonder how you are going to sort your materials."

Middle

- Move around the table, squatting next to each child, and observe if the children are sorting by one of the attributes or both (color and shape).

- Imitate what the children are doing with their materials with your own materials.

- Introduce the extra noodles for those children who may need or want more.

End

- Remind the children when they will have a few minutes left of small-group time.

- Ask the children to dump their noodles in a basket and place their ice cube trays in the center of the table. Tell them that you will be adding the materials to the toy area if they want to use them tomorrow at work time.

- Have the children move to the next part of their day by the colors of clothing they have on. You might say, for example, "If you are wearing something red, please go to the sink to wash your hands before snacktime" and so on, until all the children have transitioned.

Ideas for follow-up

- For another small-group time, have children use eye droppers and the ice cube trays to mix different colors of water.

These children and their teacher explore color mixing with colored water, ice cube trays, and eye droppers.

Developmental Range for "Sorting Noodles": Supporting Children at Different Levels

Earlier	Middle	Later
Children may	*Children may*	*Children may*
• Name colors and describe shapes but not sort the materials in any particular way. • Sort their materials by one of the attributes (color or shape).	• Notice two attributes but only sort their noodles by one. • Describe why and/or how they sorted their noodles in a particular way.	• Notice both attributes and sort their materials first by one attribute and then by the other attribute. • Explain why and how they sorted their noodles.
Adults can	*Adults can*	*Adults can*
• Listen to children's ideas and comment on what they see (e.g., "I see you have red, blue, and yellow noodles"). • Model sorting their own materials, describing while sorting (e.g., "I am putting all my red noodles in this spot and all my blue ones in this spot").	• Restate children's ideas about why and/or how they sorted their materials. • Pose simple ideas about sorting their noodles by the other attribute. For example, you might say, "I see you have all the green noodles here and the blue noodles here. I wonder if you can put all the bowtie noodles together."	• Comment on what they see children doing with their noodles. • Converse with children about their ideas and reasons for sorting their noodles in a particular way. • Pose simple ideas about sorting their materials by shape and color at the same time (e.g., "I wonder if we could put all the red round noodles in one pile and all the red twisty noodles in another pile").

Beanbag Toss

Children toss and catch beanbags made out of socks.

Time of day

Large-group time

Content areas

- Physical Development and Health

Materials

For each child and teacher:

- Beanbag made from socks (see p. 154)

Shared materials:

- Bucket

Beginning

- Pass out beanbags to the children (one beanbag per child), and ask them to toss their beanbags in the air and let them drop on the floor.

- Ask the children to toss the beanbags up in the air again but, this time, to try and catch them.

Middle

- Let the children explore tossing and catching the beanbags in their own ways.

- Comment on what you see the children doing. For example, you might say, "I see you are tossing your beanbag with one hand and trying to catch it with the other."

- Try the children's ideas yourself. For example, if you see a child tossing the beanbag with two hands, you might say, "I am going to try Hannah's idea of tossing the beanbag with both my hands," and then do the action.

End

- Bring the activity to a close by telling the children that they can try one more time to toss and catch their beanbags.

- Walk around the group with a bucket, and have children toss their beanbags in it.

- Ask a child for an idea of a way to move to the next part of your routine, and have the children move in that way to the next activity.

Ideas for follow-up

- Add some beanbags to your block area and outdoor play space.

- Use the beanbags for a recall strategy. Place area signs on buckets and have children take turns dropping the beanbags into the bucket with the area sign where they played.

Adaptations for children with special needs

- If children have difficulty catching beanbags, give them beanbags that are made with two parts as these are easier to catch.

After this small-group time, some children continued playing with the beanbags during work time, trying to toss them into buckets.

Stretching Our Bodies With Stretchy Bands

Children use elastic material to help stretch their bodies.

Time of day

Large-group time

Content areas

- Physical Development and Health

Materials

For each child and teacher:

- Stretchy bands (see p. 91, under **As part of your classroom routine**)

Shared materials:

- Upbeat instrumental music

Beginning

- Ask the children to stretch their bodies all the way up and then all the way down.

- Ask the children what other ways they can stretch their bodies, and ask them to demonstrate.

- Tell the children you have some stretchy bands that are fun to stretch with, and then distribute the stretchy bands.

- Encourage the children to explore with the stretchy bands for a short period of time.

Middle

- Put on the music you chose to use with the stretchy bands.

- Comment on what you see the children doing with the bands. You might say, for example, "I see you are using your foot to stretch your band."

- Copy the children's ideas of how to use the stretchy bands. Point out what a child is doing (e.g., say "I see you are stretching your band behind your head," and then try the movement yourself).

End

- Tell the children that the activity will be ending when the music stops.
- Ask the children to put their bands in a designated area.
- Have the children stretch their way to the next part of the classroom routine.

Ideas for follow-up

- Use the stretchy bands another day, but with slower music. Talk to the children about relaxing while they stretch their bodies.

Adaptations for children with special needs

- Loop each end of the stretchy band so that children can easily place the loops on their wrist and keep hold of the band as they manipulate it.

Stretchy bands are ideal materials for children to use during large-group time.

6
Easy-to-Make Materials

What Are Easy-to-Make Materials?

At naptime, Madison says she is not tired so her teacher brings over her "nap basket." Inside the basket are a sensory bottle and some books, including a homemade I spy book. Madison says, "I want to read that new book and look for things." She picks up the I spy book and starts to look through the pages quietly. When she is done looking through the book, she picks up the sensory bottle, rolls to her side, and quietly moves the bottle back and forth, watching the movement of the oil and water.

Some materials can be found, recycled, or purchased at a low cost, as discussed in the previous chapters. But this next set of materials includes things that you can easily make. These materials are held together and constructed by things that any teacher has: glue, tape, scissors, and your imagination! The items you need to create easy-to-make materials are simple enough to find, collect, and purchase, since you are now a professional scavenger as well.

Where Do I Add Easy-to-Make Materials in My Classroom?

Easy-to-make materials, like any materials in the preschool classroom, should be stored with similar items (e.g., chunky crayons should be placed together in the art area; a class book should be in the book area). You can provide a material in more than one

Store chunky crayons together in a bin in the art area, near other art supplies.

place or simply rotate the material into different areas. If, for example, the children are always moving the colored noodles from the house area to the toy area, you may want to just move them there.

Here are some examples of easy-to-make materials and the areas in your classroom that you might find them (step-by-step instructions for many of these materials are in the next section).

In the House Area
- Colored noodles (see p. 130)
- Play dough (see p. 150)

In the Book Area
- Puzzles (see p. 144)
- I spy book (see p. 140)
- Magnet story board (see p. 152)
- I spy bottles (see p. 153)
- Sensory bottles (see p. 155)
- Class book (see p. 155)
- Story can (see p. 48)

In the Art Area
- Chunky crayons (see p. 114)
- Rubber band paintbrushes (see p. 124)
- Play dough (see p. 150)
- Goo (see p. 151)
- Marker holder (see p. 158)

In the Toy Area
- Colored noodles (see p. 130)
- Geoboards (see p. 134 and p. 136)
- Squishy balls (see p. 142)
- Plastic bag shakers (see p. 118)

- Rain sticks (see p. 126 and p. 128)
- Magnet wands (see p. 153)
- Lego accessories (see p. 138)

In the Music Area/Shelf
- Plastic bag shakers (see p. 118)
- Rubber band guitars (see p. 122)
- Chimes (see p. 159)
- Egg shakers (see p. 159)
- Ribbon wands or bracelets (see p. 156)

In the Sand and Water Area
- Moon sand (see p. 151)

In the Block Area
- Sponge balls (see p. 116)
- Community blocks (see p. 154)
- Beanbags (see p. 154)
- Sand timers (see p. 157)
- Bowling bottles (see p. 158)

In the Outside Play Space
- Jump ropes (see p. 120)
- Wood stilts (see p. 132)

Easy-to-Make Materials in Classroom Areas

Rubber band paintbrushes in the art area

Egg shakers in the music area

Jump ropes in the outside play space

Where Do I Find Easy-to-Make Materials?

Finding easy-to-make materials is easy — you simply put on your do-it-yourself hat and put that glue and tape to work. The following pages include a step-by-step guide of easy-to-make materials. After making some of these materials, you won't be able to walk through a store, your kitchen, or school without coming up with a hundred more ideas!

Lego accessories (see p. 138) and I spy books (see p. 140) can be made for a fraction of the cost for similar products you would order online or find in a store.

Chunky Crayons

Chunky crayons are fun to color with and easy to hold for children working on their fine-motor skills.

Materials needed

- Broken crayons
- Silicone or paper cupcake holders
- Metal baking tray, cookie sheet, or cupcake pan
- Oven

Time to make

- 1½ hours (15 minutes preparation, 10 minutes to cook, 1 hour to cool in freezer [or 8 hours at room temperature])

Directions

1. Preheat oven to 375°F.

2. Remove paper labels from the broken crayons; break the crayons into small pieces; and place the sorted crayons (by similar colors) in silicone or paper cupcake holders on a metal baking tray, cookie sheet, or cupcake pan.

Copyright © 2013 HighScope® Educational Research Foundation. The owner of this book has permission to copy this page for its use in an early childhood program.

3. Fill each cupcake holder one-half to three-quarters full with the sorted crayons. (If you want marbled crayons, try mixing two or three colors, but avoid using black and brown.)

4. Place the baking tray in the oven for 10 minutes or until the crayons have completely melted.

5. Put the baking tray with the crayons in a freezer for about an hour or let cool at room temperature overnight.

6. Carefully pop out the crayons and use.

Copyright © 2013 HighScope® Educational Research Foundation. The owner of this book has permission to copy this page for its use in an early childhood program.

Sponge Balls

Children can easily catch these colorful balls made from soft sponges.

Materials needed

- New sponges (four sponges make three balls)
- String

Time to make

- 45 minutes for 20 sponge balls

Directions

1. Collect four new sponges.

2. Cut each sponge lengthwise into three equal strips.

Copyright © 2013 HighScope® Educational Research Foundation. The owner of this book has permission to copy this page for its use in an early childhood program.

3. Place a 12-inch string on the table, and lay four strips of sponge on top of each other in a crisscross pattern.

4. Tie a knot tightly in the middle so that the edges of the sponges stick out, and then make a double-knot with the string.

5. Cut excess string.

6. Arrange sponge pieces as needed. Repeat with remaining strips of sponges.

Copyright © 2013 HighScope® Educational Research Foundation. The owner of this book has permission to copy this page for its use in an early childhood program.

Plastic Bag Shakers

Plastic bag shakers create soothing, soft sounds and are easy for small hands to hold.

Materials needed

- Plastic grocery bags (one per shaker)
- Paper towel tubes (one per shaker)
- Masking tape
- Permanent marker

Time to make

- 1½ hours for 20 shakers

Directions

1. Flatten out a plastic bag; draw a rectangle; and then draw lines, dividing the rectangle into 1-inch strips.

2. Cut the handles off the bag.

Copyright © 2013 HighScope® Educational Research Foundation. The owner of this book has permission to copy this page for its use in an early childhood program.

3. Following along the lines, cut through both the top and bottom layers of the bag (be careful not to cut all the way to the top). Then cut along the side seams of bag (about the same length as the other strips).

4. Wrap what's left on the plastic bag (the part not cut) around the paper towel tube so that the strips are hanging off the paper towel tube.

5. Tape the bag to the tube with masking tape.

6. Try out your plastic bag shaker!

Copyright © 2013 HighScope® Educational Research Foundation. The owner of this book has permission to copy this page for its use in an early childhood program.

Jump Ropes

Children use these durable ropes to tie things to; drag through puddles and mud; and, of course, jump!

Materials needed

- Plastic grocery bags (18 bags for one 4½-foot jump rope)

Time to make

- 50 minutes for five jump ropes

Directions

1. Smooth out three bags in a rope-like shape.

2. Stack the three bags on top of each other, and make a knot at the top of the bags.

Copyright © 2013 HighScope® Educational Research Foundation. The owner of this book has permission to copy this page for its use in an early childhood program.

3. Braid bags.

4. As a bag runs out for the braid, take another smoothed-out bag and lay the new bag over the bag that is running out.

5. Continue braiding with the new bag and other original bags. Continue braiding in this same fashion, adding additional bags as needed.

6. After braiding all the bags, make a knot at the end.

Copyright © 2013 HighScope® Educational Research Foundation. The owner of this book has permission to copy this page for its use in an early childhood program.

Rubber Band Guitars

Children love to strum on guitars, but they are expensive and fragile. Make as many as you need of these rubber band guitars for almost no cost.

Materials needed

- Empty laundry detergent container, thoroughly rinsed
- Permanent marker
- Utility knife
- Hole puncher
- Rubber bands (about six per guitar) or plastic elastic string

Time to make

- 10 minutes for one rubber band guitar

Directions

1. Using a permanent marker, draw a rectangle on one side of the laundry detergent container. Cut out the rectangle with a utility knife.

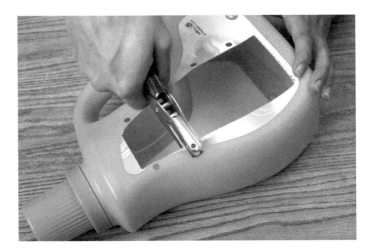

2. Punch five to six holes on each side of the rectangle with a hole puncher (holes should be parallel).

Copyright © 2013 HighScope® Educational Research Foundation. The owner of this book has permission to copy this page for its use in an early childhood program.

3. Snip one end of a rubber band.

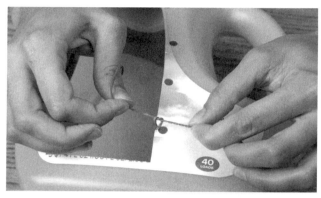

4. Tie a double-knot (or square knot) with the rubber band in a hole. (You can also use plastic elastic string instead of rubber bands.)

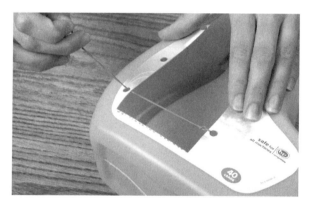

5. Pull the rubber band (or elastic string) very tight (it makes a better sound if pulled tight).

6. Tie a double-knot in the hole on the other side.

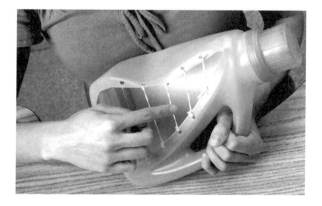

7. Repeat steps 3–6 with the remaining rubber bands to complete the strings for the guitar.

Copyright © 2013 HighScope® Educational Research Foundation. The owner of this book has permission to copy this page for its use in an early childhood program.

Rubber Band Paintbrushes

Children enjoy exploring the different paint strokes they can make with these unconventional paintbrushes.

Materials needed

- Rubber bands (12 to 15 rubber bands make one brush)
- Electrical tape
- Unsharpened pencil or dowel

Time to make

- 30 minutes for 20 paintbrushes

Directions

1. Cut one end of each rubber band. (You can also leave rubber bands whole, which creates different kinds of paint strokes.)

2. Cut a 4-inch piece of electrical tape.

Copyright © 2013 HighScope® Educational Research Foundation. The owner of this book has permission to copy this page for its use in an early childhood program.

3. Lay the rubber bands on the sticky side of the tape.

4. Place an unsharpened pencil (or dowel) on top of the rubber bands.

5. Roll the pencil (or dowel) along the tape to make a paintbrush.

6. If using the cut rubber bands, snip the ends so that the rubber bands (the "brush") are the same length.

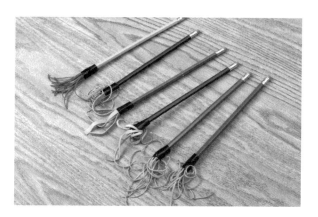

7. Repeat steps 1–6 for additional paint-brushes.

Copyright © 2013 HighScope® Educational Research Foundation. The owner of this book has permission to copy this page for its use in an early childhood program.

Rain Stick I

Just like the sounds of real rain, the sounds a rain stick makes can be mesmerizing for children to explore.

Materials needed

- Empty Pringles can or similar type of container with metal bottom
- 12-inch foil pieces (four to six pieces)
- ½ cup of dry beans or pebbles
- Electrical tape

Time to make

- 5 minutes for one rain stick

Directions

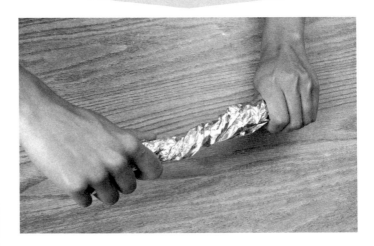

1. Twist a 12-inch piece of foil lengthwise.

2. Repeat step 1 with the remaining pieces of foil.

Copyright © 2013 HighScope® Educational Research Foundation. The owner of this book has permission to copy this page for its use in an early childhood program.

3. Put the foil pieces in an empty Pringles can (or similar type of container).

4. Add ½ cup of dry beans (or pebbles) to the container.

5. Seal the top with electrical tape (or glue).

6. Shake the can for the sounds of rain.

Copyright © 2013 HighScope® Educational Research Foundation. The owner of this book has permission to copy this page for its use in an early childhood program.

Rain Stick II

These rain sticks make soothing sounds, which can help children relax.

Materials needed

- 2 laundry caps
- Paper towel tube
- 12-inch pieces of foil (four to six pieces)
- ½ cup of dry beans or pebbles
- Hot-glue gun

Time to make

- 7 minutes for one rain stick

Directions

1. Twist a 12-inch piece of foil lengthwise.

2. Repeat step 1 with the remaining pieces of foil.

Copyright © 2013 HighScope® Educational Research Foundation. The owner of this book has permission to copy this page for its use in an early childhood program.

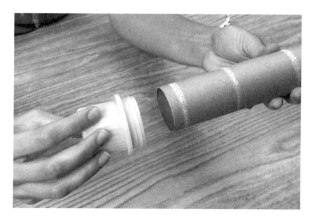

3. Glue a laundry cap on the bottom of the paper towel tube.

4. Put the foil pieces in the paper towel tube.

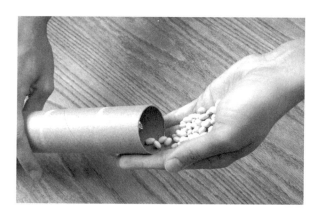

5. Add ½ cup of dry beans (or pebbles) to the paper towel tube.

6. Glue the other laundry cap to the top of the paper towel tube.

7. Shake the tube for the sounds of rain.

Copyright © 2013 HighScope® Educational Research Foundation. The owner of this book has permission to copy this page for its use in an early childhood program.

Colored Noodles

Colored noodles are so open ended that children will find lots of ways to play with this material in many different areas of the classroom.

Materials needed

- Baking pan or metal cookie sheet
- Paper towels
- Uncooked pasta (one pound of pasta makes one full bag of colored noodles)
- Food coloring
- Resealable plastic bag (gallon size)
- Rubbing alcohol

Time to make

- 8 hours (10 minutes preparation, 7 to 8 hours to dry)

Directions

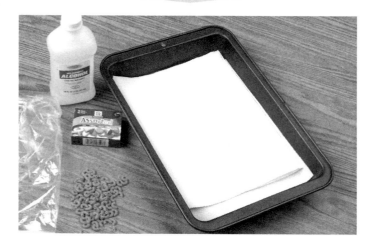

1. Line a baking pan or cookie sheet with several sheets of paper towel.

2. Put a selected amount of dry pasta in the plastic bag.

Copyright © 2013 HighScope® Educational Research Foundation. The owner of this book has permission to copy this page for its use in an early childhood program.

3. Put a few drops of selected food coloring in the bag (more pasta will require more food coloring).

4. Seal the bag, toss the pasta with the coloring in the bag, and add an additional drop or two of coloring to get the desired color.

5. Add a capful of rubbing alcohol to the bag (if making a full bag of pasta, add two capfuls of rubbing alcohol), seal the bag, and mix with your hands (rubbing alcohol sets color and helps dry out noodles).

6. Pour out pasta on paper towels to dry overnight.

Copyright © 2013 HighScope® Educational Research Foundation. The owner of this book has permission to copy this page for its use in an early childhood program.

Wood Stilts

These large-motor materials challenge children's balance and encourage their outdoor play.

Materials needed

- 2 x 4 piece of wood cut into eight 6-inch blocks (for four pairs of stilts)
- Drill
- 18 feet of rope (4½ feet of rope per stilt)
- Candle and matches

Time to make

- 1 hour to make four pairs of stilts

Directions

1. Drill a hole in the wide side of each 6-inch block of wood.

2. Pull a 4½-foot piece of rope through the hole, and then burn the edges of the rope so they don't fray.

Copyright © 2013 HighScope® Educational Research Foundation. The owner of this book has permission to copy this page for its use in an early childhood program.

3. Make an overhead knot with the rope.

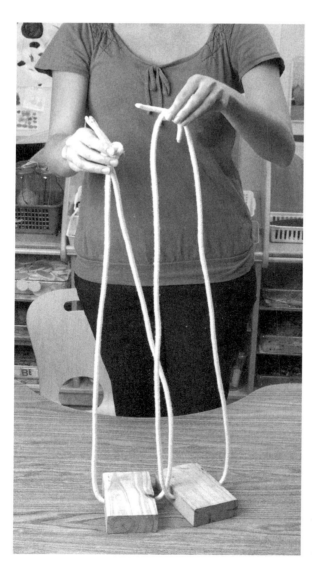

4. Repeat steps 2–3 with the remaining blocks of wood (two blocks of wood make one pair of stilts).

Copyright © 2013 HighScope® Educational Research Foundation. The owner of this book has permission to copy this page for its use in an early childhood program.

Giant Geoboard

This giant geoboard promotes collaborative play as children figure out what they can make on it together.

Materials needed

- Large piece of pegboard
- Bolts and nuts (one bolt/nut for every other hole on board)
- Different sizes of rubber bands

Time to make

- 25 minutes

Directions

1. Place a bolt through the underside of the pegboard, and twist a nut on it to secure it.

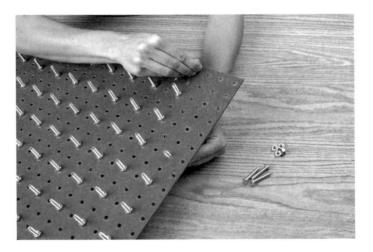

2. Repeat step 1 with the remaining nuts and bolts, placing one bolt in every other hole of the pegboard (any size pegboard works; we made ours the same size as our Lego tabletop).

Copyright © 2013 HighScope® Educational Research Foundation. The owner of this book has permission to copy this page for its use in an early childhood program.

3. Add rubber bands of different sizes so children can make shapes.

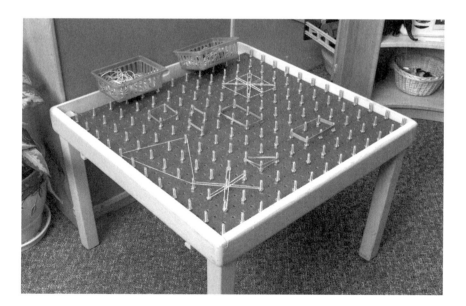

4. *(Optional)* Add the geoboard to a Lego table, and provide small containers of rubber bands along the sides of the table.

Copyright © 2013 HighScope® Educational Research Foundation. The owner of this book has permission to copy this page for its use in an early childhood program.

Small Geoboard

Using a small geoboard, children can make their own designs and shapes and develop their math and fine-motor skills as well.

Materials needed

- 8 x 8 piece of wood
- Ruler
- Pencil
- 16 nails with small heads
- Hammer
- Different sizes of rubber bands

Time to make

- 20 minutes

Directions

1. Make a 1-inch grid of dots with a ruler and pencil on an 8 x 8 piece of wood.

2. Hammer in the nails on 16 of the dots (one nail in every other dot).

Copyright © 2013 HighScope® Educational Research Foundation. The owner of this book has permission to copy this page for its use in an early childhood program.

3. Add rubber bands of different sizes so children can make shapes.

4. *(Optional)* Put baskets of small items (e.g., animals, Lego figures) near small geoboards to see how the children extend their play.

Copyright © 2013 HighScope® Educational Research Foundation. The owner of this book has permission to copy this page for its use in an early childhood program.

Lego Accessories

Lego accessories give children more ways to expand their play with Legos.

Materials needed

- Heavy paper or index cards
- Marker
- Hole puncher
- Poly (plastic) folders

Time to make

- 20 minutes for 10 pieces

Directions

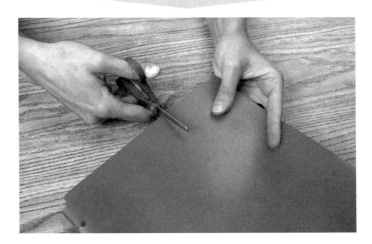

1. Cut a poly folder into different lengths and shapes (use your imagination).

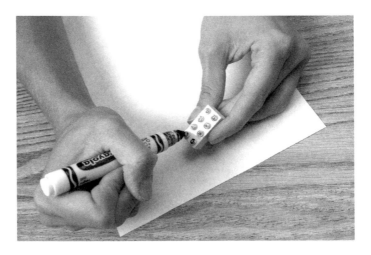

2. Use a washable marker to color the top of a Lego piece.

Copyright © 2013 HighScope® Educational Research Foundation. The owner of this book has permission to copy this page for its use in an early childhood program.

3. Press the Lego piece on heavy paper or an index card to make a pattern.

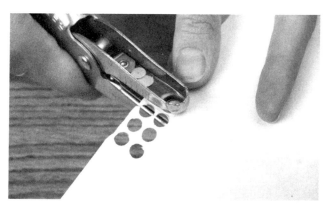

4. With a standard hole puncher, punch holes in the Lego pattern on the paper.

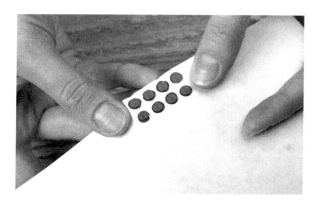

5. Align the hole-punched pattern with the Lego piece to make sure it fits.

6. Using a marker, transfer the pattern on the poly pieces by coloring in the holes.

7. Punch out the holes on the poly pieces with a hole puncher.

8. Place Lego accessories near Legos to extend children's play.

Copyright © 2013 HighScope® Educational Research Foundation. The owner of this book has permission to copy this page for its use in an early childhood program.

I Spy Book

Children love the challenge of I spy books, but they often lose interest because the store-bought books are too hard. Make these homemade versions as easy or difficult as needed so children have success in finding the items.

Materials needed

- Small collections of similar items (e.g., dinosaurs, letters, shapes, small figures)
- White paper or two pieces of white foam board
- Digital camera
- Computer
- Photo editing program
- Printer
- Photo book

Time to make

- 3 hours (for one book or multiple copies of the same book)

Directions

1. Make a white background (use two pieces of white foam board to make the background or tape white pieces of paper against a wall and on a table).

2. Create a scene with one collection of items.

Copyright © 2013 HighScope® Educational Research Foundation. The owner of this book has permission to copy this page for its use in an early childhood program.

3. Take a picture of the scene, and then take pictures of individual items in the scene.

4. Use a photo editing program to collage individual pictures into one picture or page, adding words if desired.

5. Print collaged and scene pictures, and place them side by side in a photo book.

6. Repeat steps 2–5 with another collection of items, such as letters. Have children use the collaged picture for clues of what to find in the scene picture.

Copyright © 2013 HighScope® Educational Research Foundation. The owner of this book has permission to copy this page for its use in an early childhood program.

Squishy Ball

Squishy balls are a great toy for children to help calm themselves or to use while listening to others in a group.

Materials needed

- Funnel
- ½ cup cornstarch
- Empty, dry plastic water bottle
- Water balloon

Time to make

- 5 minutes for one squishy ball

Directions

1. Use a funnel to pour ½ cup of cornstarch into a water bottle.

2. Blow up a dry water balloon to approximately 4 inches.

Copyright © 2013 HighScope® Educational Research Foundation. The owner of this book has permission to copy this page for its use in an early childhood program.

3. Stretch the balloon head over the top of the water bottle (you may need more than one person to do this).

4. Turn the bottle over, and tap/shake the cornstarch into the balloon.

5. Pinch the edge of the balloon to remove it from the water bottle.

6. Let excess air out of the balloon.

7. Tie a knot at the end of the balloon.

8. To create a classroom set of squishy balls, repeat steps 1–7.

Copyright © 2013 HighScope® Educational Research Foundation. The owner of this book has permission to copy this page for its use in an early childhood program.

Puzzles

These homemade puzzles are inexpensive to make and a favorite among children because they are about a favorite subject — themselves!

Materials needed

- Color pictures of children
- Cereal boxes or cardboard
- Glue stick
- Contact paper or laminator

Time to make

- 15 minutes for one puzzle

Directions

1. Print out color pictures of children (each picture should be about 8½ by 11 in size).

2. Cut out the backs and fronts of the empty cereal boxes (one cereal box has enough cardboard for two puzzles).

Copyright © 2013 HighScope® Educational Research Foundation. The owner of this book has permission to copy this page for its use in an early childhood program.

3. Apply glue to the cut-out rectangle (from the cereal box).

4. Glue the picture to the cardboard rectangle.

5. Trim the edges of the picture that don't fit on the cardboard.

6. Draw an X on the back of the rectangle. Alternatively, make your own template (four to eight pieces work best). See pages 147–149 for sample puzzle templates.

Copyright © 2013 HighScope® Educational Research Foundation. The owner of this book has permission to copy this page for its use in an early childhood program.

7. Laminate the puzzle (or use contact paper to cover the puzzle), and then cut your design.

8. Repeat steps 3–7 for additional pictures.

Copyright © 2013 HighScope® Educational Research Foundation. The owner of this book has permission to copy this page for its use in an early childhood program.

Template for a Four-Piece Puzzle

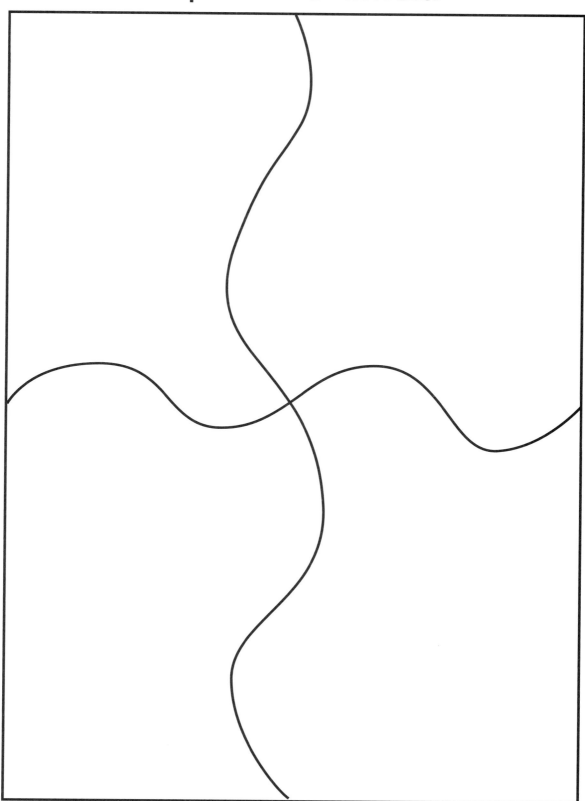

Copyright © 2013 Khululeka Community Education Development Centre. Reprinted by permission. The owner of this book has permission to copy this page for its use in an early childhood program.

Template for a Six-Piece Puzzle

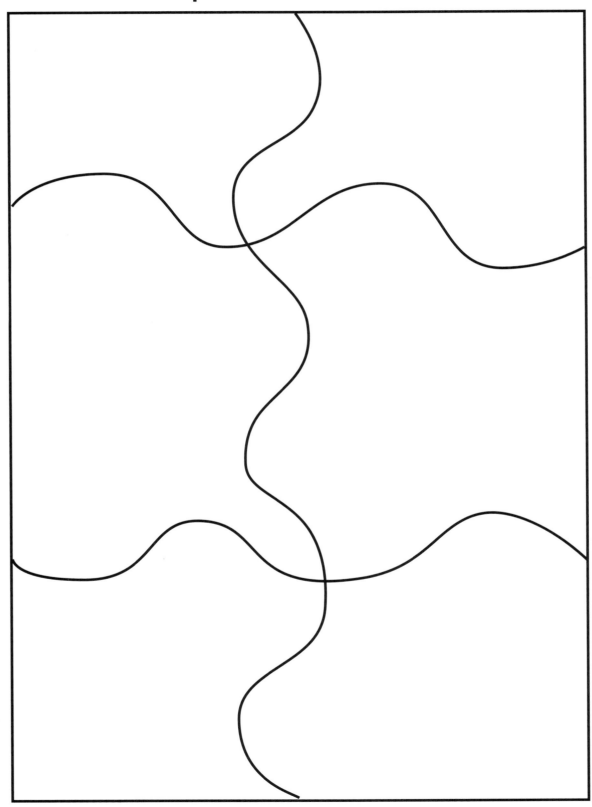

Copyright © 2013 Khululeka Community Education Development Centre. Reprinted by permission. The owner of this book has permission to copy this page for its use in an early childhood program.

Template for an Eight-Piece Puzzle

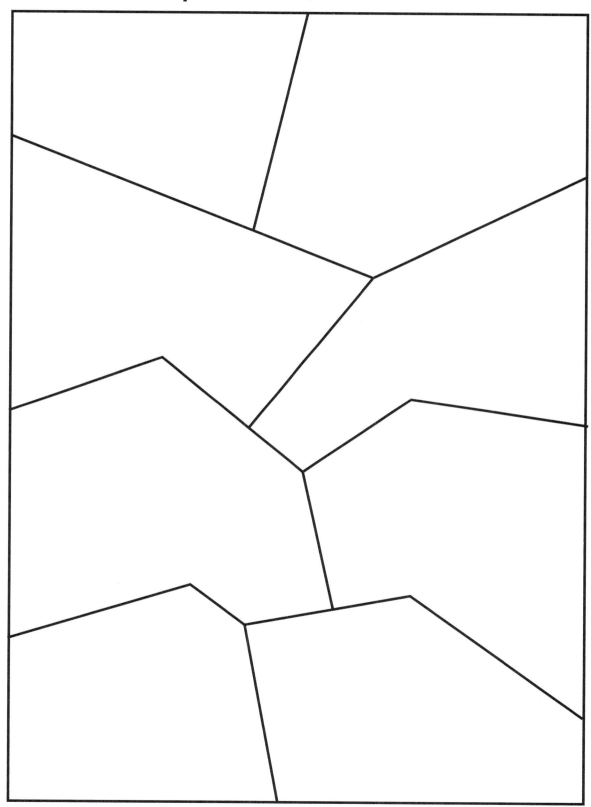

Copyright © 2013 Khululeka Community Education Development Centre. Reprinted by permission. The owner of this book has permission to copy this page for its use in an early childhood program.

Sensory Material Recipes

Play dough

Combine in saucepan:

- 1 cup flour
- ½ cup salt
- 2 teaspoons cream of tartar

Mix in separate bowl:

- 1 cup water
- 2 tablespoons vegetable oil
- 1 teaspoon food coloring

Slowly stir the water/oil mixture into saucepan.

Cook over medium heat, stirring constantly until ball forms.

Remove from heat and let cool.

Knead dough on wax paper until smooth, and store in airtight container.

Goo

Stir to combine in a bowl:

- ¾ cup warm water

- 1 cup white glue

- Food coloring (enough drops to achieve desired color)

In a second bowl, stir together:

- ½ cup water

- 2 teaspoons sodium borate (also known as Borax; found near the laundry detergents in the store)

Pour and mix water/glue mixture into the second bowl.

Store goo in a resealable plastic container or bag in the refrigerator at night (it is fine to leave it at room temperature during the day).

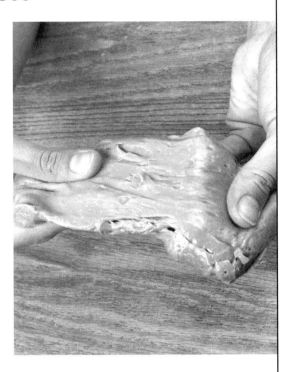

Moon sand

Mix together in a large container or bin:

- 4 cups play sand

- 2 cups cornstarch

- 1 cup water

If the mixture starts to dry out, add more water (and cornstarch, if necessary).

Other Easy-to Make Materials

Magnet story board

Directions: Cut out silhouettes of children, characters, and objects in a setting (houses, trees, etc.) from pictures, old books, or magazines. Laminate the items, and place sticky magnets on the back. Put the items in a basket next to small metal cookie sheets so children can use them as magnetic story boards.

Bright Idea
Recall Time With Magnet Story Board

For recall time, place area symbols across the top of a magnet board or metal cookie sheet (you can use a permanent marker or tape paper cutouts of symbols on the board). Pass out magnet pictures of the children in your group, and ask the children to place their picture under the area where they played at during work time and then have them recall what they did in that area.

Magnet wand

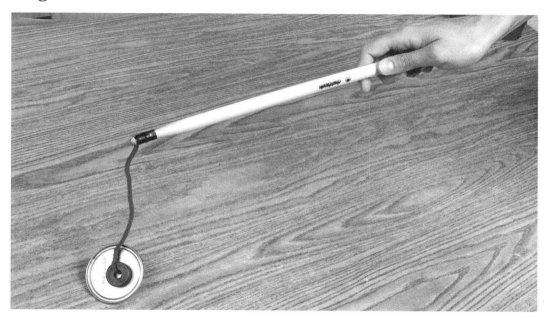

Directions: Twist a pipe cleaner around one end of a drum stick, a dowel rod, or an unsharpened pencil. Stretch electrical tape around the twisted end of the pipe cleaner to secure in place. Twist the opposite end of a pipe cleaner around a magnet.

I spy bottle

Directions: Place small, easy-to-identify items (e.g., Lego pieces, letters, numbers) in an empty, dry water bottle. Fill the remainder of the bottle with uncooked rice, and super-glue the top on.

Community blocks

Directions: Stuff different sizes of sturdy boxes (e.g., toiletry boxes) with recycled paper, and tape the boxes shut with packing tape. Take pictures of local landmarks (e.g., buildings, school), and print them out to approximate sizes of boxes. Tape each picture on a box, and use clear packing tape to cover each photo.

Double beanbag and single beanbag

Directions: To make a **double beanbag,** fill a sock with uncooked beans, and close the open end with a rubber band. Add another rubber band in the middle of the sock, creating two different sections to the beanbag. To make a **single beanbag,** fill the foot of a sock with uncooked beans, leaving enough room to sew the end. Cut off the ankle part of the sock, fold over the raw edge, and topstitch to close the seam.

Sensory bottle

Directions: Add one combination of materials (e.g., colored water with glitter and/or beads; oil and colored water; hair gel and marbles; glycerin and glitter; or liquid soap, water, and food coloring) to an empty water bottle, and then super-glue the lid on.

Class book

Directions: Choose a theme for a book (e.g., recent field trip, families in the class). Take photos related to the theme, arrange photos in a small photo album, and add words or short sentences as captions.

Ribbon wand or bracelet

Directions: Choose a holder for ribbons (e.g., paper towel tube, plastic bracelet, wooden dowel rod), and cut ribbons to desired length.

For a **paper towel tube,** punch holes to tie each ribbon in.

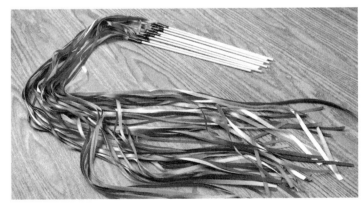

For a **plastic bracelet,** slipknot each ribbon around the bracelet.

For a **wooden dowel rod,** secure ribbons to the end of the rod with electrical tape.

Sand timer

Bright Idea
Sand Timers and Cleanup Time

To make cleanup time more fun, have children race the sand timer or see how many turns on the timer it takes them to clean up. Then ask them to try to beat the number of turns the next day.

Directions: Fill a dry, empty water or soda bottle with the desired amount of salt. Screw a tornado tube on one end and then screw another dry, empty water or soda bottle (same size as first one) on the other end.

Marker holder

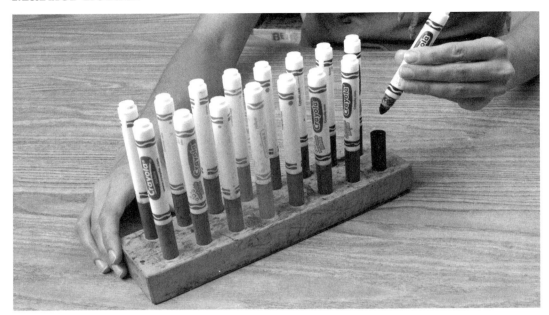

Directions: Cut a scrap piece of 2 x 4 wood to a desired length (about 9 inches for the eight basic colors). Mark 8 holes spaced out in two rows (16 holes total). Drill out holes to fit marker caps (caps should fit snug into the holes). Lightly hammer caps into the holes, and then place markers upside down into their designated spaces.

Bowling bottles

Directions: Fill bottoms of empty, dry water bottles with sand (you can mix in food or water coloring to color sand), and super-glue tops of bottles on.

Chimes

Directions: Punch holes in frozen juice lids with a hammer and nail. Pass a string through each lid, leaving ends even and untied. Tape a dowel rod along the top of a shoe box, positioning it toward the box opening. Use a utility knife to poke holes on top of the box, on both sides of the dowel rod. Pull the string with the metal lid on it through each hole and tie a knot to the desired length. Repeat so that the lids are just touching each other and strings are progressively shorter.

Egg shakers

Directions: Place a desired amount of filler (e.g., rice) into one side of a plastic egg (close the egg and shake it to experiment for your desired sound). Tape around the seam with electrical tape, making sure the tape fits tightly. Repeat with another type of filler (e.g., pebbles, beans) to create shakers that make different sounds.

What Can I Do With Easy-to-Make Materials?

In addition to adding the materials to your classroom as described earlier in this chapter, you can use these materials in other unique ways. Following are some ideas for using the things you've made in different classroom areas and during various parts of your daily routine.

Adding easy-to-make materials to classroom areas

- Add colored noodles to your art area when children are interested in gluing and collaging (see anecdote below) and then move them to your toy area when they are interested in sorting and patterning. Ask yourself, "Where else could I see children using these colored noodles?" and then place them there.

    During work time, Angie and Tomas glue colored noodles on a cardboard box and call it their "spaceship."

- Place chimes in the music area or toy area (depending on where other musical instruments are kept).

- Add community blocks, along with figures and cars, to the block area:

    Sam runs over to Lynette (his teacher) and says, "Look! It's my house. I'm going to make my whole city!" She then walks back to the block area and starts to build "her" city with the community blocks.

This young child uses small wooden figures and the class's community blocks to re-enact a recent field trip to the city's water tower.

A family book, which includes collaged pictures of the children's families, helps children develop a positive self-identity and also share a bit of themselves with classmates.

- Display class books, I spy bottles, sensory bottles, and I spy books in the book area. Children also find these materials to be comforting to look at in their nap baskets.

- Store beanbags in your block area, along with some tubs or baskets, to see what games children will create with them.

Using easy-to-make materials in your daily routine

- Save some easy-to-make materials (e.g., ribbon wands, goo, beanbags, sponge balls, shakers) for a special large-group and/or small-group time:

  During large-group time, Sandy, a teacher, hands a plastic bag shaker to each child. Then she puts on some music. "I can shake mine high," says Blaine. "I am going to shake mine low," says Courtney.

- Incorporate beanbags in your planning and recall strategies as well as during large-group times.

> **Bright Idea**
> **Plastic Bag Shakers for Planning Time**
>
> As a planning strategy, have children take turns shaking a plastic bag shaker in the area where they want to play in during work time and then tell you their plan.

- Add some of the easy-to-make materials to the classroom materials available at work time:

Eve places hollow blocks flat on the ground next to each other. She stands on top of them and strums on a guitar made from a laundry detergent bottle. She then calls out to Kelly, a teacher, and says, "Come and listen to my concert. You can sit by the stage [pointing to the blocks]."

As with all materials teachers use in the classroom, it is important to play with children in the ways they play with the materials (see "How Do I Use These Materials With Children?" on pp. 20–21 for ideas).

During large-group time, these children choose how to use their ribbon bracelets while listening and moving to lively music.

Activities for Easy-to-Make Materials

Bowling for Bottles

Children bowl with bowling bottles and a soft ball.

Time of day

Small-group time

Content areas

- Mathematics
- Physical Development and Health

Materials

For each child and teacher:

- Set of bowling bottles (about three or four per child; see p. 158 for directions)
- Soft ball or tennis ball

Shared materials:

- None

Backup materials:

- Paper
- Pencils
- Extra bowling bottles

Beginning

- Ask the children if they have ever bowled before, and encourage children who have to share what they remember about their experiences with bowling.

- Show children the bowling bottles and soft ball. Say "Today we are going to bowl!"

- Tell the children that they will need room to bowl and therefore will not stay at their table for small-group time. With the children, move to another predetermined area (a large, open space in your classroom or outside [weather permitting]).

Middle

- Show the children how to bowl by rolling the soft ball, knocking down some bottles, and then counting how many bottles you have knocked down.

- Pass out the materials to the children so they can start.

- Support children's different stages in counting by commenting on what you see the children doing. For example, you might say, "Keith, I see you knocked down two bottles and there is one still standing."

- Help children count by pointing to each bottle as they say the numbers.

- Offer paper and pencils to children who are ready for an extension. Encourage them to "keep score" by placing tally marks on the paper (which is also a great way to encourage counting).

- Offer children extra bottles if they want an additional challenge.

End

- Ask the children to put all their bottles and balls in designated spaces.

- Transition the children to the next part of the daily routine by their ages. For example, say "If you are three years old, please go to the door and get ready for outside time," "If you are four years old….," and so forth until all the children have transitioned.

Ideas for follow-up

- Add bowling bottles to your block area or outdoor play space.

Support children's understanding of numbers by encouraging children to use their fingers (or other objects) while counting out loud.

Developmental Range for "Bowling for Bottles": Supporting Children at Different Levels

Earlier	Middle	Later
Children may	*Children may*	*Children may*
• Knock the bowling bottles over without counting.	• Count some of the bottles but not be able to tell how many.	• Count all their bottles and then say how many they have.
• Say random numbers as they look at their bottles or say they knocked over some, all, or no bottles.	• Count all their bottles using one-to-one correspondence (e.g., point to each bottle when counting).	• Count their bottles standing and then say how many they knocked down (e.g., "I have two bottles left standing, so I knocked down two bottles").
• Rote count as they look at their bottles (i.e., say numbers in sequential order but not point to each bottle when counting).		
Adults can	*Adults can*	*Adults can*
• Comment on what they see children doing (e.g., "I see you knocked over three bottles").	• Copy children's actions with their set of materials and model counting bottles using one-to-one correspondence (e.g., "I knocked down three bottles. One [touch the first bottle], two [touch the second bottle], and three [touch the third bottle]").	• Listen to children as they count and comment on their findings.
• Point to the bottles as children say the numbers aloud.		• Make comments that encourage children to extend their mathematical thinking (e.g., "I wonder how many you have left since you knocked two down").
• Restate children's comments about how many bottles they knocked over.		
• Count with children, reminding them to say one number for each bottle.	• After children count the bottles, say the total number that they have (e.g., "You counted two — you knocked down two bottles").	

Painting With Rubber Bands

Children explore the paint strokes they can make with rubber band paintbrushes.

Time of day

Small-group time

Content areas

- Creative Arts
- Physical Development and Health

Materials

For each child and teacher:

- Rubber band paintbrush (see p. 124 for directions)
- Small plate of paint
- Smock

Shared materials:

- Large sheet of butcher paper

Backup materials:

- Rubber band paintbrushes made from rubber bands of different widths and lengths

Beginning

- Say something like "Today we will be using some different kinds of paintbrushes."
- Show the children the rubber band paintbrushes, and ask them about what kinds of lines or marks they think these paintbrushes will make.

Middle

- Have children put on smocks, give each child a paintbrush and plate of paint, and encourage them to explore their new paintbrushes on the large sheet of butcher paper.
- Use your own paintbrush as the children are using them, and describe what you are doing. For example, you might say, "I am going to move my brush back and forth like Mikey is doing."
- Walk around the table (or on the floor, if that is where the paper is), and converse with children about what they have discovered with the brushes.
- Pass out the backup brushes to children who might want them.

End

- Have the children place their brushes in a sink or tub of water, hang up their smocks, and wash their hands.

This young girl experiments with the different strokes she can make with a rubber band paintbrush.

- Tell children that you will add these new brushes to the art area tomorrow for work time.
- As children are done washing their hands and cleaning up, ask them to move in a different way (e.g., jump, hop, skip) to the next part of your routine.

Ideas for follow-up

- Have children paint with other open-ended materials, such as corks, leaves, or string.

Adaptations for children with special needs

- Some children may find it easier to use a thicker pencil, so make sure some of the paintbrushes are made with thicker pencils.
- To strengthen children's fine-motor abilities, make some paintbrushes with golf-sized pencils (pencils that are about three inches in length).

Developmental Range for "Painting With Rubber Bands": Supporting Children at Different Levels

Earlier	Middle	Later
Children may	*Children may*	*Children may*
• Explore with the paint-brush, making random strokes. • Describe their actions in one or two words (e.g., "Back and forth").	• Try to move their brush to get a particular result. • Describe the marks their brush is making.	• Intentionally use the brushes in some way. • Compare the strokes made by two or more brushes. • Describe their brush strokes in more detail.
Adults can	*Adults can*	*Adults can*
• Copy children's actions with their own brushes. • Describe children's actions in a sentence (e.g., "You are moving your brush back and forth, which is making lines on the paper").	• Make the same brush strokes as the children are making with their paintbrushes. • Converse with children about their ideas and descriptions of brush strokes.	• Copy children's ideas with their brushes. • Comment on children's paintings and converse about why and how the strokes are different (e.g., "I see you are twisting your brush; it makes a circle shape"). • Pose simple, open-ended questions about why something happened (e.g., "I wonder why that brush makes thin lines and this one makes thick lines?").

Shake to the Music

Children have a parade using plastic bag shakers.

Time of day

Large-group time

Content areas

- Creative Arts
- Physical Development and Health

Materials

For each child and teacher:

- Plastic bag shakers (see p. 118 for directions)

Shared materials:

- Marching music

Beginning

- Ask the children if they have ever seen a parade before. Listen to their ideas about what things they have seen in a parade.
- Ask the children to show you what marching looks like, and then practice marching with them.

Middle

- Tell the children that you would like to have a parade around the classroom.
- Pass out the shakers, and encourage the children to show you how they could use them in the parade.
- Put on the marching music, and lead the children around the classroom.
- Ask different children to lead the parade.

End

- Tell the children that you are going to have one more parade around the classroom, but this time you are going to march to the next part of your daily routine.
- Ask the children to place their shakers in a designated spot near the location of the next part of your daily routine.

Ideas for follow-up

- Have a parade with all the different kinds of shakers that you have made.

Popping With Sponge Balls

Children make sponge balls "pop" by shaking a parachute.

Time of day

Large-group time

Content areas

- Physical Development and Health

Materials

For each child and teacher:

- Sponge ball (see p. 116 for directions)

Shared materials:

- Parachute

Beginning

- Explain to the children that today you have some balls to use with the parachute.
- Lay out the parachute, and tell the children to find a loop to hold on to.
- Ask the children to shake the parachute fast and then slow.
- Add the sponge balls to the parachute.

Middle

- Shake the parachute fast and slow again with the sponge balls on it.
- Ask the children for their ideas on how to shake the parachute (e.g., high, low, crazy low to the ground and then up high after the count of three).

End

- Tell the children that you are going to shake the parachute in one more way.
- After the last way, ask the children to put the parachute back on the floor and sit on top of it.
- Have the children move to the next part of their daily routine by the color on the parachute that they are sitting on (e.g., "If you are sitting on yellow, you can wash your hands for snacktime") until all the children have transitioned.

"How high can we make the sponge balls pop?" asks this teacher, as the children shake the parachute higher and higher.

Ideas for follow-up

- Add the sponge balls to the block area for children to use.

- Repeat this activity with music (look for instrumental music that has an interesting beat).

- Use plates and sponge balls at another large-group time, encouraging children to explore different ways they can use these two materials together.

7

Involving Families

Why Family Involvement Is Important

Involving families in the classroom is important for many different reasons. When families are involved, parents understand the learning that is taking place in the class, the family's culture is represented more fully in the classroom, children and families have greater feelings of comfort when it comes to school, and teachers build relationships with families and community.

Prominent early childhood authors, researchers, and organizations back up what we, as teachers, already know intuitively about the positive effects of family involvement. According to Alice Honig (2002), when parents show confidence in their teachers and learning environments (and this confidence grows when parents are involved), their children are more likely to feel confident in their learning environment as well. Amy Baker and Lynn Manfredi/ Petitt (2004) note that positive relationships between families and teachers allow "communication to flow naturally and seamlessly…each child is better understood, and the care between home and center is seamless" (p. 18). The National Association for the Education of Young Children believes that family involvement is so important that one of its six standards for early childhood professionals directly addresses building family and community relationships (National Association for the Education of Young Children, 2009b).

For these reasons, I suggest putting on your community hat and getting families involved in your learning environment in as many ways as you can.

How to Get Families Involved

So now you understand why it *is* important to have families involved, but *how* do you get them involved? One way to encourage family involvement is to hold family meetings about once a month. During such a meeting, families come into the school or classroom and talk and learn about different topics, which can vary from curriculum areas, such as literacy or math, to power struggles in the grocery store — whatever is helpful to your families. You can also use these family meetings to create classroom materials.

Family involvement is a key component in a child's early educational success. Participating with the children in large-group time, talking with a teacher at pickup time, or reading a story at dropoff time are just few of the ways families can become involved in the classroom.

Before you organize monthly family meetings, make sure your meetings are held at a time and on a day when most families can attend. To find out this information, send home a simple survey asking families about their availability. (If you have families whose home language is not English, find someone who can help translate written materials.) To encourage parental attendance, offer parents child care for their children in another room and/or provide dinner (ask for donations for pizza or have a potluck). Making these meetings meaningful and welcoming to parents will help ensure that they will be repeat attendees.

Incorporating the materials from this book in your classroom may bring many questions from family members; for example, "Why are my kids playing with rocks?" or "I am paying a lot of money for this school, so why is my child playing with paper towel tubes?" These are valid questions. As teachers, we want to educate our families so that they can see the value of open-ended materials in the classroom and in the home; a parent workshop (see p. 177) should help parents understand why we use open-ended materials.

The rest of this chapter includes "tools" to help you encourage family involvement in your program, including a parent workshop, a sample letter to send to families, and suggestions on how to have a successful (and fruitful) "making materials for the classroom" family meeting.

A Parent Workshop: Why Is My Child Playing With Paper Towel Tubes?

Workshop activity	Agenda	Materials
Welcome	Welcome parents and introduce yourself.	Nametags
Objectives	In this workshop we will • Discuss what open-ended materials are. • Identify why open-ended materials are important in the classroom and at home.	Objectives written on chart paper or whiteboard
Opening activity	Pass out some closed-ended materials to parents to try and use. Give parents about 5–10 minutes to "play" with the materials. Walk around and facilitate like you typically do with their children. Pass out open-ended materials for parents to play with. Give parents the same amount of time to use these materials. Walk around and facilitate as you typically do with their children. As a whole group, discuss which materials were more interesting to use.	Closed-ended materials (e.g., lacing cards, jack-in-the-box, coloring pages, board games) Open-ended materials (e.g., play dough and rocks; paper plates and balls; beans and different-sized containers; string and various recycled things, such as tubes to put on the string)

Workshop activity	Agenda	Materials
Opening activity (cont.)	Ask parents to discuss what they learned while using the closed-ended materials, and write their ideas on chart paper or the whiteboard.	Chart paper or whiteboard, marker
	Ask parents to discuss what they learned while using open-ended materials, and write their ideas on chart paper or the whiteboard. (Be sure to point out the learning that you saw when parents used the materials, and the different ways parents used the same open-ended materials.)	Chart paper or whiteboard, marker
Main ideas	Explain the differences between open-ended and closed-ended materials.	
	Closed-ended materials	
	• Usually perform one task.	
	• Can only be used in one way, the "right" way.	
	• Have a right and wrong way to use them.	
	Open-ended materials	
	• Can be used in many ways.	
	• Promote imagination and creativity.	
	Show some pictures of (or actual) materials for parents to look at and decide if they are open or closed ended.	Pictures of (or actual) open- and closed-ended materials

Workshop activity	Agenda	Materials
Main ideas (cont.)	Ask parents to list some materials around their homes that are open ended that their children could play with.	Paper, pencils
	Explain that we want children to use open-ended materials at school and at home, because they	Pictures of children using open-ended materials in fun and interesting ways in the classroom
	• Promote imagination and creativity.	
	• Encourage problem-solving skills.	
	• Create sustained interest because they can do so many different things.	
	• Provide many different textures and properties that children can explore in their own ways.	
	• Can be cheaper and not as many of them are needed, because children will use them in a variety of ways.	
Application	Ask parents to list some toys that their children like to use at home.	Paper, pencils
	Have parents share their list with the group and express if they think those are open or closed ended.	Chart paper or whiteboard, marker
At home	Have parents think of some open-ended materials that their children could use in their home, and then share their ideas as a whole group.	Chart paper or whiteboard, marker

Now that families have a better understanding of why you have these types of materials in the classroom, you can start asking them to collect things. You can use the family letter home (p. 182) or use the template (p. 183) to make your own.

A Family Meeting: Making Easy-to-Make Materials

Why not put materials right into your families' hands, and get some made for the classroom at the same time? Invite families in for a parent meeting, and advertise that they will be making some materials for the classroom (and some to take some home to use with their children!).

Before the family meeting

Collect all the items needed to make the materials first, before the family meeting. Then set up stations in the classroom (one station per material) with the following:

- Clear, printed directions (see chapter 6 for directions; make sure each station has several copies of the directions)

- Necessary items for making the material

- Completed sample material

- Total number of the material you need (be sure to include one for each family to take home)

During the family meeting

Ask families to split themselves into small groups and find a station to work at (be sure to have enough stations so that people are not crowded).

At the end of the family meeting

When your meeting is coming to a close, thank parents for their time and let them collect one of each of the materials to take home. Talk with parents about how easy this was, and ask them to share ideas of materials they can make (with their children) for their homes.

As the school year progresses, you might discover more materials that are needed in your classroom — don't be afraid to ask your parents to collect these materials for you. Parents really enjoy being a part of the classroom and helping in different ways. You can also host another meeting to make materials. You might even discover some parents that are willing to make materials on their own!

At the end of this family meeting at the HighScope Demonstration Preschool, the children join their parents for a snack of popcorn and juice.

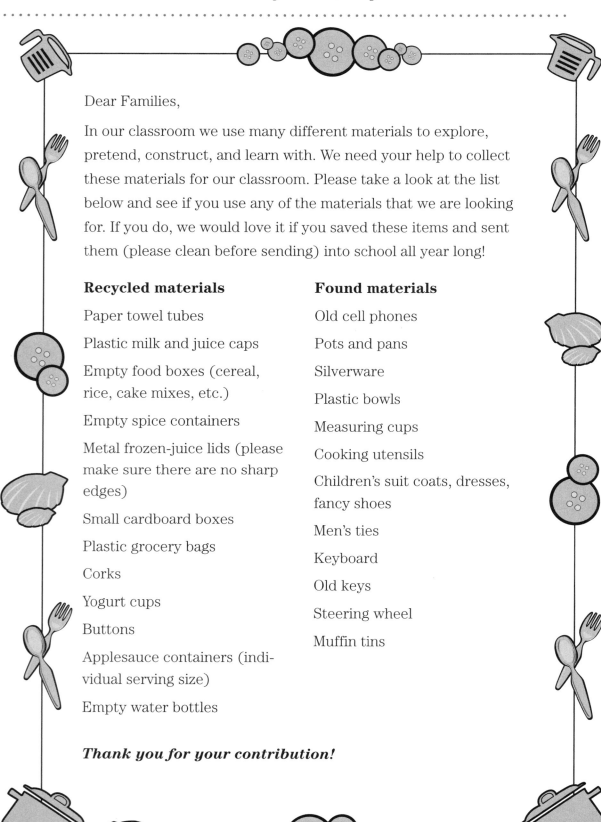

Dear Families,

In our classroom we use many different materials to explore, pretend, construct, and learn with. We need your help to collect these materials for our classroom. Please take a look at the list below and see if you use any of the materials that we are looking for. If you do, we would love it if you saved these items and sent them (please clean before sending) into school all year long!

Recycled materials

Paper towel tubes

Plastic milk and juice caps

Empty food boxes (cereal, rice, cake mixes, etc.)

Empty spice containers

Metal frozen-juice lids (please make sure there are no sharp edges)

Small cardboard boxes

Plastic grocery bags

Corks

Yogurt cups

Buttons

Applesauce containers (individual serving size)

Empty water bottles

Found materials

Old cell phones

Pots and pans

Silverware

Plastic bowls

Measuring cups

Cooking utensils

Children's suit coats, dresses, fancy shoes

Men's ties

Keyboard

Old keys

Steering wheel

Muffin tins

Thank you for your contribution!

Copyright © 2013 HighScope® Educational Research Foundation. The owner of this book has permission to copy this page for its use in an early childhood program.

Dear Families,

In our classroom we use many different materials to explore, pretend, construct, and learn with. We need your help to collect these materials for our classroom. Please take a look at the list below and see if you use any of the materials that we are looking for. If you do, we would love it if you saved these items and sent them (please clean before sending) into school all year long!

Recycled materials   **Found materials**

Thank you for your contribution!

Copyright © 2013 HighScope® Educational Research Foundation. The owner of this book has permission to copy this page for its use in an early childhood program.

References

Baker, A. C., & Manfredi/Petitt, L. A. (2004). *Relationships, the heart of quality care: Creating community among adults in early care settings.* Washington, DC: National Association for the Education of Young Children.

Epstein, A. S. (2012). *Language, literacy, and communication.* Ypsilanti, MI: HighScope Press.

Epstein, A. S., & Hohmann, M. (2012). *The HighScope Preschool Curriculum.* Ypsilanti, MI: HighScope Press.

Henderson, A. (1991). *Make believe.* Play Activities Series. London: Pre-school Learning Alliance National Centre.

HighScope Educational Research Foundation. (2011). *Adult-child interaction participant guide.* HighScope Preschool Workshop Series. Ypsilanti, MI: HighScope Educational Research Foundation.

Honig, A. S. (2002). *Secure relationships: Nurturing infant/toddler attachment in early care settings.* Washington, DC: National Association for the Education of Young Children.

Marshall, B. (2008). A day in the life of an open-ended material. *HighScope Extensions, 22*(3): 3. Available at the HighScope *Extensions* archive: http://www.highscope.org/Content.asp?ContentId=209

National Association for the Education of Young Children. (2009a). *Developmentally appropriate practice in early childhood programs serving children from birth through age 8* (Position statement). Retrieved from http://www.naeyc.org/files/naeyc/file/positions/position%20statement%20Web.pdf

National Association for the Education of Young Children. (2009b). *NAEYC Standards for Early Childhood Professional Preparation Programs* (Position statement). Retrieved from http://www.naeyc.org/files/naeyc/file/positions/ProfPrepStandards09.pdf

Rose, D. L. (2011, June 15). The tipping point of rocks [Web log post]. Retrieved from http://www.howtosmile.org/blog/posts/tippingpoint

Materials Index

About the Author

Emily Thompson is a public elementary school teacher in Dexter, Michigan. She previously taught in the HighScope Demonstration Preschool in Ypsilanti, Michigan, and is a certified HighScope trainer. Emily writes articles for HighScope's curriculum newsletter, *Extensions,* and facilitates online courses. She wrote *Planning Around the Preschool COR* (HighScope Press, 2011) and served on the team that developed the HighScope key developmental indicators, which form the content of the HighScope Preschool Curriculum. Emily credits her knowledge about children and what they need developmentally to these experiences. She says that she "learned *what* to teach in college and *how* to teach from HighScope."